Float Analysis
Powerful Technical Indicators
Using Price and Volume

A Marketplace Book

Float Analysis
Powerful Technical Indicators
Using Price and Volume

Steve Woods

John Wiley & Sons, Inc.

Published by John Wiley & Sons, Inc., New York.
Published simultaneously in Canada.

This publication is designed to provide accurate and authoritative information in regard to the subject matter covered. It is sold with the understanding that the publisher is not engaged in rendering professional services. If professional advice or other expert assistance is required, the services of a competent professional person should be sought.

ISBN 0-471-21553-8

Printed in the United States of America.

10 9 8 7 6 5 4 3 2 1

To the woman who lit up my life and convinced me that anything was possible, my wife, Martha. And to the two beautiful daughters she gave me, Catherine and Toby.

"Most good ideas sparkle in simplicity."

— Estée Lauder

Table of Contents

Acknowledgments

My heartfelt thanks to Jean and Kenneth Wentworth who encouraged and supported my market efforts.

Also a special thanks goes to Jan Arps — my mentor, business partner, and friend — who encouraged me to document my discoveries and place a high value on them.

I especially thank Peter Seitel whose clarity of thinking helped me confront the most pertinent ideas in this book. In addition, I thank Janice Fain Dean, Cheryl Morden, Mary Leonard, Gordon Rothrock, Bill Fix, and David Wentworth, who helped in the editing process. A special thanks also goes to Rich Doyle, who was always there to listen and support me in whatever I did.

I would also like to thank my publishing attorney, Nina Graybill, as well as Chris Myers and Jean Eske at Marketplace Books for making the publishing process a smooth and easy one. Also, I would like to thank proofreader Joan E. Gordon and book designer Mary Ann Stavros-Lanning for such excellent work.

In addition, a special thanks for making the stock market come alive goes to William O'Neil, who founded *Investor's Business Daily* and wrote *How to Make Money in Stocks*. Mr. O'Neil, you are a great light to the investment world.

Thanks also to all my market teachers who took the time to write down their ideas — Ted Warren, Nicolas Darvas, Jesse Livermore, Robert Edwards, John Magee, Benjamin Graham, David Dodd, Gustave Le Bon, Bernard Baruch, Peter Lynch, Martin Zweig, Martin Pring, Gerald Loeb, Stan Weinstein, Victor Sperandeo, and especially to W.D. Gann, whose ideas truly made float analysis possible.

Introduction

W. D. Gann: The Inspiration for Float Analysis

When I first studied the stock market in earnest, two short passages in W.D. Gann's *Truth of the Stock Tape*[1] had a profound impact on the way I looked at price and volume charts. In the first passage, Gann talked about the amount of volume it took for a stock to make a 23-point move to the upside. He said that 1.6 million shares traded hands, which was "five or six times the floating supply." In the second passage, he talked of a stock in which the shares were "changing hands about twice each week." From these passages, I realized that Gann had a unique way of looking at a stock's trading volume. He was treating a company's tradable shares as a whole unit, and he was tracking them as they changed hands one or more times. The moment I read these ideas, I had an epiphany that developed into what I call *float analysis*.

The insight seemed simple. I had seen and was fascinated by many high-flying stocks that rose in price to amazing heights only to come crashing down to earth. Using Gann's idea, I imagined a company's shares as a changing unit in time — a distance on a chart in which all the shares traded once. Now I imagined that what probably happened to those high-flying stocks was that a less-than-savvy group of investors bought the shares right at the top. With no one else to sell to — they were stuck. Next I pictured the price dropping below this float turnover at the top. With overhead supply above the price, this would be a great time to sell.

---

1 Gann, W.D. (1976). *Truth of the Stock Tape*, Lambert-Gann Publishing, Pomeroy, WA.

To test my idea, I hired Jan Arps to write what is now known as the Woods Cumulative-Volume Float Indicator. Jan, a successful 30-year veteran of the commodity and stock markets, develops trading software as an Omega Research solution provider. Using the software that we developed, I could hardly contain myself with the results of my studies. My insight was entirely accurate. Every stock that made a top had a float turnover right at the peak, followed by a sell signal as the price dropped below those who were "stuck at the top."

As an introductory example, Cyprus Semiconductor (CY), is shown in figure i-1. During the nine weeks at the top, the cumulative trading volume equaled the number of shares in the float. (The nine-week period is framed by two lines and a dot which will be explained in chapter 1.)

As I continued my research, I made a second discovery of equal importance to the first: every stock making a bottom always has a float turnover right at the base (also discussed in chapter 1). These discoveries seemed so profound and yet so elementary that they demanded to be documented. So Jan and I co-authored an article titled "Float Analysis" for the magazine

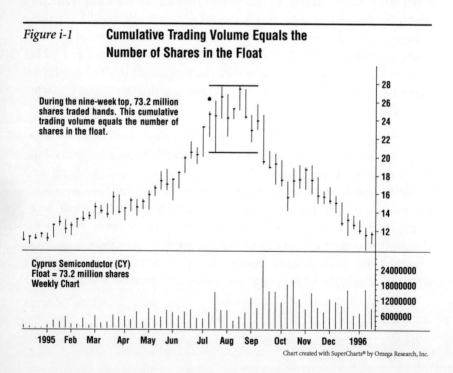

Figure i-1 **Cumulative Trading Volume Equals the Number of Shares in the Float**

During the nine-week top, 73.2 million shares traded hands. This cumulative trading volume equals the number of shares in the float.

Cyprus Semiconductor (CY)
Float = 73.2 million shares
Weekly Chart

Chart created with SuperCharts® by Omega Research, Inc.

Technical Analysis of Stocks and Commodities (December 1996). In the months that followed its publication, my phone was constantly ringing. I talked with brokers, floor traders, fund managers, and investors from all over the globe who wanted to know more about my discoveries. This book is the response to all of their inquiries and my attempt to clarify and expand the ideas that originally appeared in that *Stocks and Commodities* article. It is my contention that these ideas are not only of major significance in the history of technical stock analysis but that they will change the way technicians look at price and volume charts. When viewed without the float, a price and volume chart is an incomplete picture showing only two-thirds of what one is actually looking at. This book is my attempt to show the whole picture. I believe that anyone who takes the time to study these ideas will benefit from them greatly.

I know I have benefited from these ideas. As I will discuss at the end of Chapter One, in the 16 months from September 1998 to January 2000, I took a small account of a few thousand dollars and grew it tenfold. My primary methods and tools are found in this book. To everyone who loves to study stock charts, I hope this new approach will be as exciting and profitable for you as it has been for me.

— Steve Woods

Float Analysis
Powerful Technical Indicators
Using Price and Volume

CHAPTER ONE

Watching the Float:
The New Look of Price and Volume Charts and Their Relationship to a Stock's Future Price Direction

. . . for the world wasn't flat; it was actually round.

Float analysis is a holistic approach to studying the technical behavior of stocks. By this I mean it treats the shares actually being traded as equal in importance to *price* and *volume* activity.[2] Thus, price and volume are seen as only two-thirds of the picture, with the number of shares actually traded being the final third that completes the picture. The power of looking at stocks this way is that it demonstrates a direct relationship between the volume of shares traded in the past and subsequent future movements in price. Thus, *float analysis* is a powerful tool to predict future stock price movements. In addition, by studying stocks holistically, float analysis expands and clarifies the definition of several technical terms. These include *bottoms* and *tops, support* and *resistance, and accumulation* and *distribution.*

Float analysis also allows us to create a model of price, volume, and tradeable shares activity. As a model it does not claim to be the "truth" of all stock price and volume activity. It is, of course, just one point of view among many. But

---

2 In preparing this book, I have undertaken the challenge of writing to as wide an audience as possible. To make the process easier for the beginners I have bold italicized technical terms that may need further explanation. Definitions are found in the glossary.

1

like any valid model, it has the ring of truth; and to all who listen, float analysis rings rather loudly. Its appeal as a model of stock behavior is three-fold. First, it is based on several discoveries that are easy to understand. Second, it is backed up by hard data. And third, it makes common sense.

The first and most important discovery, made in 1993, is a simple concept with profound implications. In order to understand this discovery, we need to know two key terms: *float* and *float turnover*. The float is well known to knowledgeable market players. I coined the term *float turnover* to explain the discovery.

The Float

Any given stock has only a certain number of shares that are actually available for trading. These freely traded shares in the hands of the public are called the float, a shortened version of the ***floating supply of shares***. For big companies, like Intel or Microsoft, the number can be over a billion shares. For a small, obscure company, it may be a few hundred thousand. But every company has a specific number of shares that is actually traded by the public. The float should not be confused with the ***shares outstanding***, which includes both the floating supply of shares and those shares held tightly by the company's management. The float number for any given company can change periodically; the management might issue more shares, they might sell their shares, or the shares might go through a stock split. The number of shares in a company's float is not a secret. It is a publicly accessible number provided by several sources.[3]

A Float Turnover

A float turnover is the amount of time it takes for a number of shares to trade that cumulatively corresponds with the number of shares in the stock's float. For example, if a company's float has 100 million shares that are actively trading and the total cumulative volume of shares traded over

---

3 The sources I use to find a stock's float number are the chart service *Daily Graphs* (1-800-472-7479), the Yahoo! Internet financial page (http://quote.yahoo.com), and *Investor's Business Daily* (1-800-831-2525).

the last year was 100 million shares, then a single float turnover would be a one-year span starting from the current date and going back to the day when the cumulative total of the volume equaled 100 million shares. In other words, all we've done is add the volume numbers from a starting point back to a date when the total equals the float number.[4]

There is in this definition an important point that needs to be noted. Although the company's float is 100 million shares and 100 million shares were traded in a one-year span, we cannot say that all the shares in the float have been traded. This is because it is impossible to know the intentions of all the market participants. There may be short-term *day traders* who buy and sell several times during a float turnover, and there may be long-term investors who are holding their shares and not trading at all. This being the case, we can only say *approximately* all the shares in the float were traded. We can, however, quite correctly say that the total number of shares that were traded corresponds to the number of shares in the stock's float. This is because we can add up the number of shares that were traded during any time frame and compare it to the stock's float number. When the number of shares traded in any time frame is the same as the float number, we can say that by our definition we have a float turnover.

To some degree, a complete change of ownership in the company is **implied** by a float turnover, but it can never be measured with any degree of precision.

The Float Turnover as a Formula

Since a single float turnover occurs when a stock's *cumulative trading volume* is equal to its floating supply, we can determine how many float turnovers have occurred within a given period of time simply by dividing

---

4 With the implementation of the Riskless Principle Rule on February 1, 2001, the New York, American and NASDAQ stock exchanges all calculate volume of shares traded in the same manner. Thus if 100 shares are traded between two investors, the volume is reported as simply 100 shares. Prior to this date, the NASDAQ market practiced a 'double counting' of shares. Because the book was written before the change, all calculations take this double counting into account. Float Analysis studies the transfer of stock from one party to another. Thus I preferred the NYSE and AMEX method and I welcome the change that NASDAQ finally made. When analyzing NASDAQ stocks for this book, I adjusted the numbers so that 100 shares traded between two parties is seen as 100 shares and not twice the amount."

the float number into the time frame's cumulative trading volume. To see this as a formula, let FT stand for float turnover; let CTV stand for cumulative trading volume; and let F be the number of shares in the stock's float.

$$\text{X number of float turnovers} = \frac{\text{Cumulative trading volume over any given time span}}{\text{Number of shares in the float}} \qquad FT = \frac{CTV}{F}$$

EXAMPLE:

$$FT = \frac{\text{10 million shares (CTV)}}{\text{10 million shares in the stock's float (F)}} \qquad FT = 1$$

The First Discovery

The first and most important discovery in float analysis is

absolute bottom formations and *absolute top formations* always contain a single float turnover with a *valid breakout trading point*. In addition, single float turnovers with a valid trading point can be found at *consolidation areas* at all price levels.

An absolute bottom or an absolute top refers to the historically lowest *bottom formation* or the historically highest *top formation* that occurs on charts with turnaround price moves. A valid breakout trading point is a buying or selling opportunity that would have made you money had you taken the position.

Look at any stock you care to study. If it has made a turnaround price move after a long *up-trend* or a long *down-trend*, a single float turnover with a valid breakout trading point will be found right at the bottom or right at the top. This is an extremely powerful idea with profound trading implications.

> A single float turnover with a valid breakout trading point will be found right at the bottom or right at the top. This is an extremely powerful idea with profound trading implications.

So you can thoroughly understand these ideas, I'll devote the rest of the chapter to explaining them. First, I'll present them in a model graphic form. Following this, I'll examine the price and volume chart of one company's float turnover history over a seven-year period. To conclude the chapter, a simple random sample experiment will confirm just how commonplace these formations are. In chapter 2, I'll give a complete list of 10 specific float analysis discoveries that I have made. These are based on my initial discovery, and they create a foundation for the float analysis model of stock behavior. In subsequent chapters, greater detail and discussion will be combined with numerous examples to explain and expand these ideas.

Scenario One — The Smart Money and the Losing Money

To be easily explained, good ideas need an example. To that purpose, imagine two groups of investors. One very savvy group I'll call "the smart money folks." The other group is less than savvy, and I'll call them the "losing money crowd." Now picture a company whose stock has gone down from $55 to $22. The company is having a temporary setback in its product pipeline but actually has a bright future ahead of it. The losing money crowd is — yes, losing money. They bought at the wrong time and are selling at the wrong time. Instead of buying low and selling high, they bought high and are now selling low. The very act of their selling is driving the price lower, and they're bailing out because they fear the falling prices.

While this is happening, the smart money folks are evaluating the company's fundamental value. They believe that the company has a promising future and that the lower price merely means that the stock is going on sale at a fantastic bargain-basement price. Now just for the sake of this story, let's pretend that the smart money folks are able to accumulate the *entire* floating supply of available shares. Let's say that as they are buying it, the

Figure 1-1 | Scenario One

Showing a float turnover in which the total number of shares that trade at the bottom corresponds with the number of shares in the float

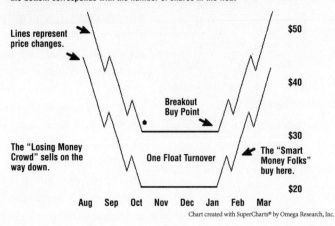

Lines represent price changes.

Breakout Buy Point

The "Losing Money Crowd" sells on the way down.

One Float Turnover

The "Smart Money Folks" buy here.

$50
$40
$30
$20

Aug Sep Oct Nov Dec Jan Feb Mar

Chart created with SuperCharts® by Omega Research, Inc.

Figure 1-2 | A Float Turnover Right at the Bottom

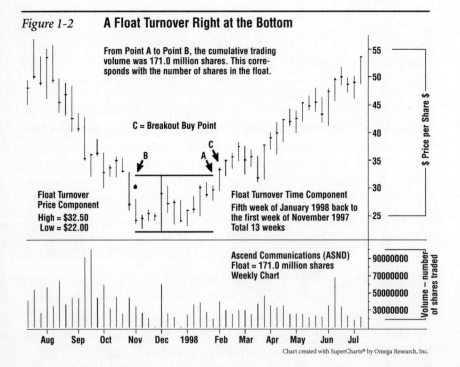

From Point A to Point B, the cumulative trading volume was 171.0 million shares. This corresponds with the number of shares in the float.

C = Breakout Buy Point

B

C

A

Float Turnover Price Component

High = $32.50
Low = $22.00

Float Turnover Time Component

Fifth week of January 1998 back to the first week of November 1997
Total 13 weeks

Ascend Communications (ASND)
Float = 171.0 million shares
Weekly Chart

55
50
45
40
35
30
25

$ Price per Share $

90000000
70000000
50000000
30000000

Volume – number of shares traded

Aug Sep Oct Nov Dec 1998 Feb Mar Apr May Jun Jul

Chart created with SuperCharts® by Omega Research, Inc.

stock's price goes sideways in a trading range between $32 and $22. The smart money folks have now taken an excellent position and control the ownership of the entire float. As expected, the company's temporary set-back passes, and because the smart money folks are holding all tradable shares, the price begins to rise back toward $55. From a technical point of view, the smart money folks have become a *base of support* from which prices will rise. In poker terminology, they're holding a great hand and anyone who wants to play will have to pay to see 'em.

While this story is complete fiction, something quite close to this actually occurs. Stocks that decline from high price levels to low price levels only to turn around and go back up always have a single float turnover (implying new ownership of the stock) with a valid trading point right at the bottom of the turnaround price move. A graphic representation of this model scenario would look like figure 1-1.

Commonly Asked Questions

The idea of a float turnover at the bottom of a turnaround price move and the graphic that illustrates it always generate numerous questions, so let me try to answer the most common ones first.

Do graphs of real stocks actually look like the graph in Scenario One?

Yes! I'll discuss several such stocks in later chapters and in appendix A, which includes a compendium of examples of stocks exhibiting float turnover for-mations. The fictional graphic in Scenario One was actually created from the chart of Ascend Communications (ASND) (see figure 1-2).[5]

What are the key components of a float turnover?

Since a float turnover is the foundation of float analysis, let's be clear about it. A float turnover has two components — a *time component* and a *price*

---

5 If you are new to chart reading, the chart of Ascend Communications is a weekly chart. The top portion of figure 1-2 contains weekly price bars. Each bar shows the highest and lowest price for any week on the chart. The cross mark on the bar indicates the closing price for that week. The vertical histogram lines at the bottom of the chart show how many shares were actually traded during that week. For example, in the second week of June 1998, over 70 million shares were traded and the price reached a high near $50 and a low of around $46, and it closed the week near its high of $50.

component. The time component refers to a specific time frame in which the total number of shares traded corresponds with the number of shares in the float. The price component refers to the range of prices, highest and lowest reached, during the specified time frame. In figure 1-2, Ascend's float turnover occurs during the three months of November, December, and January, so the time component is three months. The range of prices during this time was between $22 and $32.50.

What are the black dot and two horizontal lines?

The black dot and two horizontal lines mark the time and price components of the float turnover, respectively. The time element begins with point A, the fifth week in January 1998, and extends backward to the black dot, which is placed above the first week of November 1997. Point B marks the end of the count. Within this 13-week time frame, the total number of shares traded equaled the 171.0 million shares in the float of Ascend Communications. The two horizontal lines represent the price component of the float turnover. They mark the highest and lowest prices reached during the entire float turnover. The highest price reached is $32.50 and the lowest is $22. The lines stretch the entire distance so that we get a better visual sense of the entire float turnover, and they also serve as *trigger lines* for buy and sell signals — to be discussed in later chapters.

If you have the two lines, why do you need the black dot?

When the first indicator used in float analysis was invented,[6] I wanted to know which *price bar* in the past showed me where the cumulative volume equaled the company's float number. The dot was created to show that bar in the past. When I told Jan Arps that I wanted to know when the stock's price got above or below the float turnover, he recommended the two horizontal trigger lines at the highest and lowest points in the float turnover. Thus, the dot and two lines were created.

---

6 There are three indicators used in float analysis. They were created and developed by Jan Arps, a trading software developer and certified Omega Research solution provider, and me. The indicators are the Woods Float Indicator, the Woods Float Percentage Indicator, and the Woods Float Channel Indicator. These indicators are discussed at length in chapter 3.

Although the dot may not seem to be necessary, it actually confirms that the two trigger lines have gone the complete cumulative volume distance needed to equal the stock's float. If a stock comes public and trades for quite some time without enough cumulative trading volume, the software will not be capable of plotting the two lines in their entirety. Thus, the dot confirms that the cumulative backward count was successful.

Scenario Two — The Yin and Yang of Float Analysis

In float analysis the saying "as below, so above" is completely accurate. Like the Taoist yin/yang symbol, everything in float analysis has a mirror image counterpart. In Scenario One, we looked at a bottom formation. Now in Scenario Two, we'll look at its inverse: a top formation. All the ideas are basically the same except they're reversed. Once again, let's start with a piece of fiction and talk smart money and dumb money. This time, we have a stock that is making a beautiful increase in price from $12 to $48.

> In Scenario One, we looked at a bottom formation. Now in Scenario Two, we'll look at its inverse: a top formation. All the ideas are basically the same except they're reversed.

The smart money folks bought at the bottom and on the way up and now recognize that the stock's fundamentals do not justify the present high valuation level. In a trading range between $38 and $48, they start to sell to none other than the losing money crowd. This crowd has watched the price rise and are hoping that the stock is heading much higher. They loved the look of the chart as prices moved up and can only visualize higher prices to come. Now imagine that every single available share in the floating supply is distributed to the losing money crowd, and once they're holding them, there's no one left who wants to pay a higher price. The price starts to drop, and they're stuck in *losing positions*. From a technical standpoint, the losing money crowd has just become what's called a *ceiling of resistance* or *overhead supply*. What this means is that the price has dropped below where they got in, and if it comes back up to near where they bought it, they'll probably sell just to break even. This potential for selling is a deterrent to higher prices. In our fictional scenario, the stock even-

Figure 1-3

Scenario Two

Showing a float turnover in which the total number of shares that trade at the top corresponds with the number of shares in the float

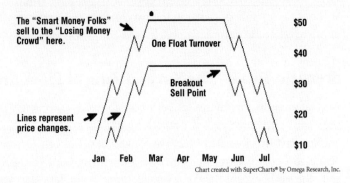

The "Smart Money Folks" sell to the "Losing Money Crowd" here.

One Float Turnover

Breakout Sell Point

Lines represent price changes.

$50
$40
$30
$20
$10

Jan Feb Mar Apr May Jun Jul

Chart created with SuperCharts® by Omega Research, Inc.

Figure 1-4

A Float Turnover Right at the Top

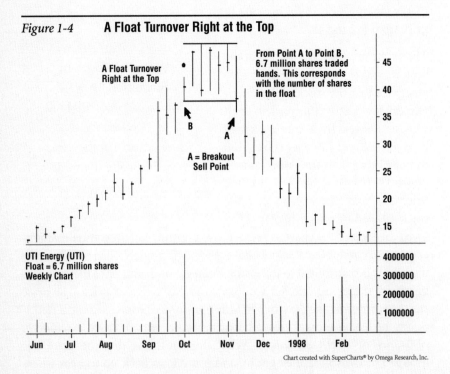

A Float Turnover Right at the Top

From Point A to Point B, 6.7 million shares traded hands. This corresponds with the number of shares in the float

B

A

A = Breakout Sell Point

45
40
35
30
25
20
15

UTI Energy (UTI)
Float = 6.7 million shares
Weekly Chart

4000000
3000000
2000000
1000000

Jun Jul Aug Sep Oct Nov Dec 1998 Feb

Chart created with SuperCharts® by Omega Research, Inc.

tually comes all the way back to $12 as the losing money crowd bails out and drives the price down.

As in Scenario One, this story is complete fiction; but again, something close to this actually occurs. Stocks that rise to high levels only to come back down in price have one complete float turnover (implying a change in ownership) with a sell signal trading point right at the top. A graphic representation of this model scenario is seen in figure 1-3. As in the first scenario, our model of price action is based on an actual stock. Here the stock used was UTI Energy (UTI) (see figure 1-4).

More Commonly Asked Questions

How did you know where to begin adding the volume numbers together?

There is no specific day to begin adding volume numbers because a stock's float turnover gets recalculated every day, much like a moving average. The software that makes float analysis possible allows us to discover where various float turnover formations occur in a stock's trading history. After noticing that Ascend's chart pattern had formed a big U shape and that UTI Energy had formed an upside-down U shape, I used the software to discover where the float turnover occurred at the bottom and the top, respectively.

Considering that long-term investors may never trade their shares and short-term traders may be trading more than once, it seems rather hard to believe that the number of shares traded at a bottom consolidation area is equal to the number of shares in the float! How is this possible?

One way to look at it is that the float turnover is just a simple cumulative total of shares traded within certain time boundaries; the number of shares in question has to fit somewhere at the bottom. To illustrate this idea, look at figures 1-5, 1-6, and 1-7. Each chart represents the weekly trading history of three fictitious companies — ABC Inc., LMNOP Inc., and XYZ Inc.

All three charts are exactly alike in terms of price and volume behavior. Their prices came down from $50 to $20 and then went back to $50. The volume numbers are also alike, and they are fixed at exactly 12 million shares for each week. This is highly unlikely, but it serves a purpose, as

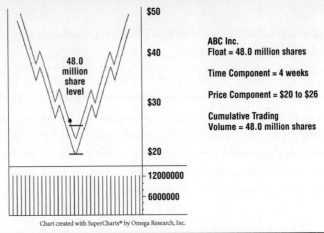

Figure 1-5   **The Precision Profit Float Indicator—ABC Inc.**

48.0 million share level

ABC Inc.
Float = 48.0 million shares

Time Component = 4 weeks

Price Component = $20 to $26

Cumulative Trading
Volume = 48.0 million shares

Chart created with SuperCharts® by Omega Research, Inc.

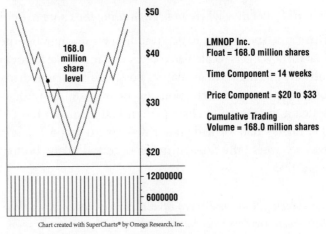

Figure 1-6   **The Precision Profit Float Indicator—LMNOP Inc.**

168.0 million share level

LMNOP Inc.
Float = 168.0 million shares

Time Component = 14 weeks

Price Component = $20 to $33

Cumulative Trading
Volume = 168.0 million shares

Chart created with SuperCharts® by Omega Research, Inc.

Figure 1-7   **The Precision Profit Float Indicator—XYZ Inc.**

288.0 million share level

XYZ Inc.
Float = 288.0 million shares

Time Component = 24 weeks

Price Component = $20 to $42

Cumulative Trading
Volume = 288.0 million shares

Chart created with SuperCharts® by Omega Research, Inc.

you'll see. Now notice that the float numbers are different for each company. ABC Inc. has only 48 million shares in its float, LMNOP Inc. has 168 million shares in its float, and XYZ Inc. has 288 million shares in its float. Now notice that each company's float turnover fits right at the bottom of each chart. We can see this quite clearly because the weekly volumes are exactly 12 million. Thus, what differs between them is the amount of time it took for the cumulative trading volume to equal each company's float. ABC Inc. has the smallest float, so its float turnover is just four weeks long and fits tightly at the bottom of the chart. LMNOP Inc. has a float of 168 million, and it takes 14 weeks for the cumulative trading volume to equal the float number. The last company, XYZ Inc., has the largest float, requiring 24 weeks for the float turnover to occur. Thus, for each stock the float turnover fits neatly at the bottom of its chart. Another explanation is that the lack of trading by long-term investors and the frequent trading by short-term traders cancel each other out, and what remains is a close approximation of a complete change in the ownership of the stock.

How is it possible that these ideas are new in the stock market? They seem to make such common sense, you'd think it would be a rather well-known idea.

The fact that no one has noticed or written about this phenomenon **is** rather amazing. I think it is likely that some professionals have used these ideas but have kept them as part of their trading secrets. I also believe that these observations have been made possible by the advent of personal computers. Before computers, keeping track of the number of shares traded was an incredibly difficult task because of the sheer volume and size of the numbers that had to be calculated. If you're tracking by hand, the float turnover of even a couple of large cap stocks with floats in excess of one billion shares you will be incredibly busy. With personal computers and great charting software like Omega Research's TradeStation and SuperCharts, the necessary calculations are done in seconds, making new discoveries possible.

The Common Sense Ring of Truth

The idea that float turnovers with *breakout* points occur right at the bottom or right at the top has a common sense ring to it. I say this more than just figuratively because, when I share this idea with anyone who knows nothing about the stock market, their eyes inevitably light up and they say

"Wow, yeah, I get it. The smart money folks buy the shares in the float at the bottom, then they're tightly held and the price rises. Then when prices are at the top, the losing money crowd buys them all and the price drops. It makes perfect sense."

The Importance of the Discovery of Float Turnovers at Bottoms and Tops

With these graphics and stock examples, I have presented the first two of 10 specific discoveries concerning stock behavior using float analysis. These first two discoveries are:

1. Single float turnovers with a valid breakout buy point always occur at absolute bottom formations.
2. Single float turnovers with a valid breakout sell point always occur at absolute top formations.

To the best of my knowledge, I am the first to write about these discoveries, and their importance cannot be overstated. The reason for this is simple. The sooner a position can be taken after a sound base of support occurs, the earlier one will be able to take advantage of large price moves. Likewise, the earlier one can recognize a ceiling of resistance, the greater the likelihood of minimizing losses. If sideways consolidation price moves commonly last one float turnover in length, then we should be able to measure this and make surprisingly accurate predictions as to a new upward or downward price move that is about to take place.

Everyone agrees that the key to success in the stock market is maximizing profits and minimizing losses. Now we have an excellent tool to achieve those goals: float analysis.

In Search of a Breakout Buy Point: A Case History of Xicor

Float turnovers should be thought of as similar to a moving average. A stock's float turnover is a constantly changing phenomenon. It gets replotted each day by adding today's volume with all previous days' volume until the cumulative total equals the float number. This means that the size and shape of the turnover changes from day to day. It's this constantly changing nature of float turnovers that allows us to see various patterns or formations of support and resistance as well as giving us buy and sell signals.

To better understand how they generate buy and sell signals and allow us to find excellent trading opportunities, let's now look at another example of a stock that made a long-term bottom only to turn around and rise back to its original level. Instead of just locating the float turnover at the very bottom of the chart, I'm going to track the float turnovers as they changed during the stock's trading history. Seeing how the float turnover is plotted at different points in a step-by-step process will demonstrate how the software searches for a valid breakout buy point.

A Case History

Xicor Inc. (XICO)
Float = 16.4 million shares[7]

Look at the chart of Xicor in figure 1-8. From 1989 to 1995, the price moved from the $8 level down below $1 and back up to $8. It forms a large U shape on the chart.

Now let's study its float turnover as it changes from bar to bar on the chart. Figure 1-9 shows the first float turnover that can be plotted. I have added two vertical dashed lines to the float turnover so that it now is in the shape of a rectangle. These dashed lines serve no purpose other than that of a visual aid to help us picture the entire float turnover and how it changes from bar to bar. They will also be helpful later when I discuss using *channel lines* as a second way of viewing float turnovers.

In figure 1-9, note that the top horizontal line is at the highest price level during the float turnover and the bottom line is at the previous lowest float turnover level. The price at point A has penetrated this lower line. Realize that the top and bottom horizontal lines not only serve to show us the high and low levels of a float turnover but they also serve as triggers to show

---

7 Although I hardly ever trade in junk heap stocks under $10, I chose this example because, to the best of my knowledge, Xicor's floating supply of shares during the time span studied remained at 16.4 million shares with little variation. This makes it ideal for study purposes.

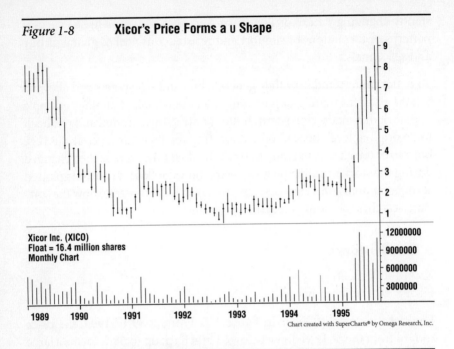

Figure 1-8 **Xicor's Price Forms a ∪ Shape**

Xicor Inc. (XICO)
Float = 16.4 million shares
Monthly Chart

Chart created with SuperCharts® by Omega Research, Inc.

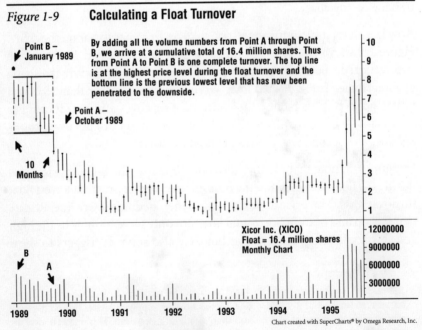

Figure 1-9 **Calculating a Float Turnover**

Point B –
January 1989

By adding all the volume numbers from Point A through Point B, we arrive at a cumulative total of 16.4 million shares. Thus from Point A to Point B is one complete turnover. The top line is at the highest price level during the float turnover and the bottom line is the previous lowest level that has now been penetrated to the downside.

Point A –
October 1989

10
Months

Xicor Inc. (XICO)
Float = 16.4 million shares
Monthly Chart

Chart created with SuperCharts® by Omega Research, Inc.

when the price has moved above or below a float turnover. Thus, if the price penetrates a horizontal line, the horizontal lines get recalculated to the new level on the next bar.[8] The two horizontal lines on figure 1-9 extend from January 1989 to October 1989. During those 10 months, 16.4 million shares were traded, which corresponds with the number of shares in Xicor's float. This was determined by simply adding up the volume of shares traded until 16.4 million shares were reached.

It is quite important to understand just how these lines can change as we recalculate the float turnover at various points. So that these changes are properly understood, I'm going to show five charts of Xicor with float turnovers plotted at different points. Figures 1-10, 1-11, 1-12, 1-13, and 1-14 show the float turnovers at these five different points as the price of Xicor was sliding down from the $8 level. Viewing these charts in this sequence shows how the lines can change when we do our calculation at different starting points.

The Relationship of a Stock's Price to Its Current Price Range Is an Important Consideration in Float Analysis

Most of these charts have something in common that is important to note. In each case but one, the price at point A is either near the bottom line or piercing through it. In other words, pricewise, it's at the low end of the float turnover range. The one that is different is figure 1-12, where the price rallies briefly and approaches the top line. The *rally*, though, is short-lived, and the price once again heads downward.

In float analysis, the present price in relation to the current *float turnover price range* is an important consideration.

---

8 Let me further explain: It will appear on certain bars and in particular breakout trading points that the lines representing the highest and lowest points are not actually plotted at the highest and lowest points of the float turnover and thus seem inaccurate. The reason for this is that we want to be alerted to buy and sell signals that occur when the price breaks above or below a current float turnover price range. Thus, if on a particular bar the price penetrates through the existing top or bottom lines of a float turnover, the price is shown as going through that line. Then on the next consecutive bar, the high and low price range is replotted at the new level. This allows us to see quite clearly when the price is moving above or below a pre-existing float turnover. It also allows the lines to serve as triggers that generate buy and sell signals.

Figure 1-10   Rate of Turnover = 13 Months

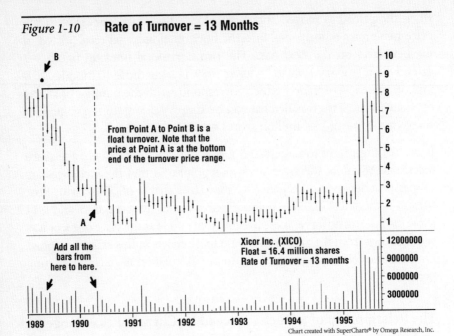

From Point A to Point B is a
float turnover. Note that the
price at Point A is at the bottom
end of the turnover price range.

Add all the
bars from
here to here.

Xicor Inc. (XICO)
Float = 16.4 million shares
Rate of Turnover = 13 months

Chart created with SuperCharts® by Omega Research, Inc.

Figure 1-11   Rate of Turnover = 16 Months

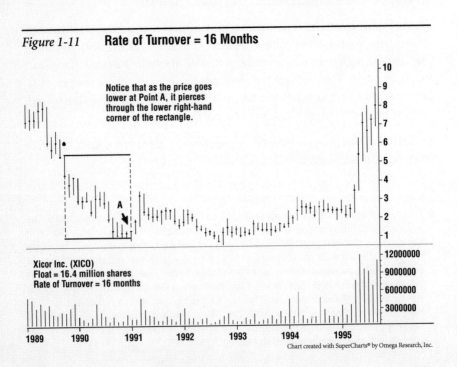

Notice that as the price goes
lower at Point A, it pierces
through the lower right-hand
corner of the rectangle.

Xicor Inc. (XICO)
Float = 16.4 million shares
Rate of Turnover = 16 months

Chart created with SuperCharts® by Omega Research, Inc.

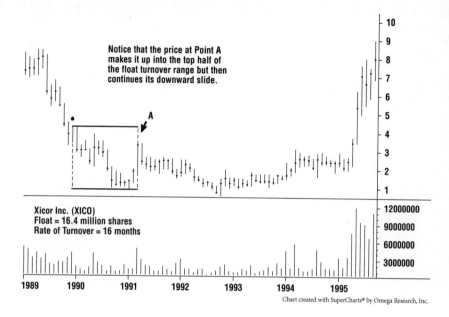

Figure 1-12 **Rate of Turnover = 16 Months**

Notice that the price at Point A makes it up into the top half of the float turnover range but then continues its downward slide.

A

Xicor Inc. (XICO)
Float = 16.4 million shares
Rate of Turnover = 16 months

Chart created with SuperCharts® by Omega Research, Inc.

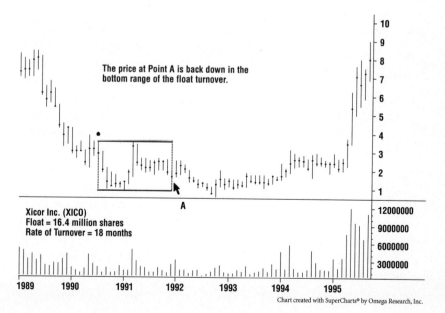

Figure 1-13 **Rate of Turnover = 18 Months**

The price at Point A is back down in the bottom range of the float turnover.

A

Xicor Inc. (XICO)
Float = 16.4 million shares
Rate of Turnover = 18 months

Chart created with SuperCharts® by Omega Research, Inc.

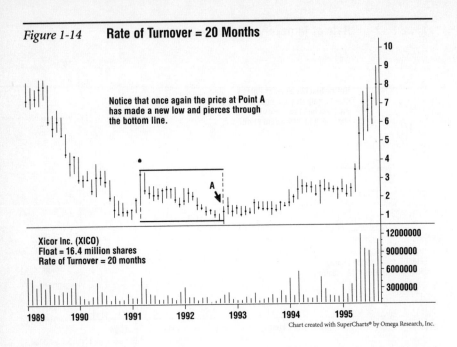

Figure 1-14   **Rate of Turnover = 20 Months**

Notice that once again the price at Point A has made a new low and pierces through the bottom line.

A

Xicor Inc. (XICO)
Float = 16.4 million shares
Rate of Turnover = 20 months

1989   1990   1991   1992   1993   1994   1995

Chart created with SuperCharts® by Omega Research, Inc.

If today's closing price of a stock is at the bottom of a float turnover range, then everyone who bought above today's price made a bad decision because they're holding losing positions. If the price is to move upward, it must work its way through plenty of investors who might want to sell just to break even.

> **Float analysis beautifully and simply shows us where this transition occurs: the valid breakout buy point.**

Thus, we have a ceiling of resistance or overhead supply above the current price. On the other hand, if today's closing price is above the float turnover range, everyone who bought in the trading range made a good decision. Now the stock has a base of support underneath it. This base of support is created by those buyers who have accumulated the stock and are holding their shares at a profit. Thus, a stock going down in price has overhead supply causing resistance to an *upward move*, and a stock going up in price has support below as it rises. A stock that was going down in price but turns around and goes up must have a point at which the overhead resistance turns into accumulation support. Float analysis beautifully and simply shows us where this transition occurs: the valid breakout buy point.

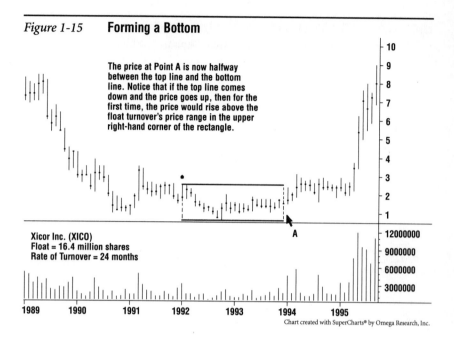

Figure 1-15   **Forming a Bottom**

The price at Point A is now halfway between the top line and the bottom line. Notice that if the top line comes down and the price goes up, then for the first time, the price would rise above the float turnover's price range in the upper right-hand corner of the rectangle.

Xicor Inc. (XICO)
Float = 16.4 million shares
Rate of Turnover = 24 months

A

Chart created with SuperCharts® by Omega Research, Inc.

Resistance to Support — The Valid Breakout Buy Point

Returning to our charts of Xicor, in figure 1-15 we see that something new is beginning to happen. The top and bottom lines are not as far apart, and the price is about halfway between them.

As we look at figure 1-16, we see a most fascinating event: the ceiling of overhead resistance changes to a base of support! The top line has moved down and the price has moved up, crossing above it. This is a critical moment in the history of the stock. For this stock, it is a valid breakout buy point. In other words, buying the stock here will be profitable.

The stock is now supported by the buyers underneath the price at this break-out buy point. The buying that took place from May 1992 to December 1993 has become a base of support from which the stock's price can rise. During these months, the stock was being accumulated by a group of savvy investors, those smart money folks, who recognized its value. Since they are holding their shares tightly, the price rises. From this point, it ascends back to the $8 level. This breakout buy point represents a first for this series of charts because it is the first time that the price gets above the highest price in

Figure 1-16 **The Moment of Transition from Overhead Resistance to Accumulative Support**

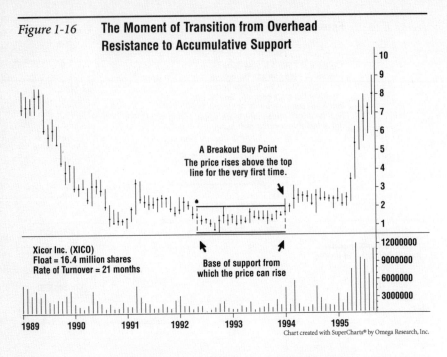

A Breakout Buy Point
The price rises above the top line for the very first time.

Xicor Inc. (XICO)
Float = 16.4 million shares
Rate of Turnover = 21 months

Base of support from which the price can rise

Chart created with SuperCharts® by Omega Research, Inc.

Figure 1-17 **The Ceiling of Overhead Resistance Changes to a Base of Support**

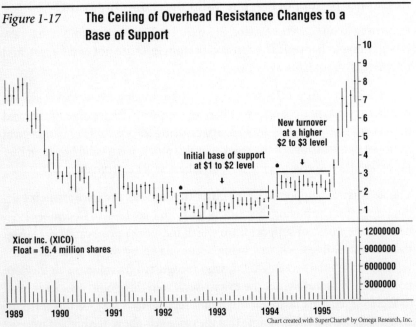

New turnover at a higher $2 to $3 level

Initial base of support at $1 to $2 level

Xicor Inc. (XICO)
Float = 16.4 million shares

Chart created with SuperCharts® by Omega Research, Inc.

the range of the changing float turnovers. During the stock's decline, prices were piercing the float turnover's bottom horizontal line to the downside. Now for the first time, they have crossed the top horizontal line to the upside.

A Word of Caution

It is important to note that we are looking at the behavior of this stock in hindsight. This has several implications. If we'd been tracking it while it was forming a bottom and had bought the stock at the breakout buy point just mentioned, there would have been no guarantee that it was a valid breakout and about to rise as it does in this example.

As we'll see in chapter 4, breakout points are not always valid breakouts. It is quite possible for a stock to break above the float turnover and then *move to the downside* instead of the upside. We said earlier that in float analysis everything has a yin/yang quality. This also applies to buy and sell signals. In chapter 2, I will show two common formations where a buy signal looks like a sell signal and a sell signal looks like a buy signal.

It is easy to get excited about stock methods such as float analysis and assume they are guaranteed cash cows that spew out money with little effort on the part of the analyst. Instead, it's important to recognize that float analysis and its indicators are tools to help the thoughtful analyst discern bottoms and tops as well as bases of support and ceilings of resistance.

Changing Ownership Implied at Various Price Levels

Sometimes after a float turnover with a breakout buy point forms at a bottom, the price will rise somewhat and then go sideways to form a new base of support at a higher level. It would seem that the owners at the lower level are selling to the people at the higher level, thus implying a change of ownership from one level to the other. Looking again at our example, we see that this is exactly what happens with Xicor. The initial base of support is in the $1 to $2 range—then the stock's price rises to the $2 to $3 consolidation range and again has a single float turnover with a valid breakout buy point (see figure 1-17).

From this $2 to $3 range, the stock's price rises to the $6 to $8 level. When the price breaks above the $3 level, we have a second buying opportunity as once

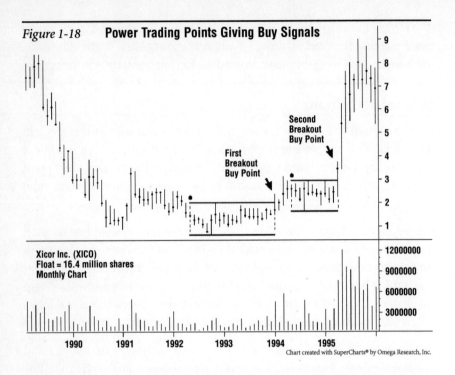

Figure 1-18   **Power Trading Points Giving Buy Signals**

Second Breakout Buy Point

First Breakout Buy Point

Xicor Inc. (XICO)
Float = 16.4 million shares
Monthly Chart

1990   1991   1992   1993   1994   1995

Chart created with SuperCharts® by Omega Research, Inc.

again a breakout buy point occurs. From here the price rises quite rapidly (see figure 1-18).

Obviously something is happening with this company to create such a rally. A look at its earnings reports in *Standard and Poor's Daily Stock Price Record* shows that the company had started to turn a profit in 1994, coinciding with the stock's initial breakout above its absolute bottom float turnover range. In the first quarter of 1995, the company reported earnings per share growth of 133%. After this report, the price rallied.

Now two questions come to mind: "How many shares were traded in this run to the upside?" and "Does the stock have another float turnover at this $6 to $8 level?" The answer to both questions is interesting. The distance of the move in price from the $2 to $3 level up to the $8 to $9 level is a float turnover in length. Then another float turnover occurs in a sideways price pattern at the top (see figure 1-19).

Our next chart of Xicor Inc. shows these formations properly labeled (see figure 1-20).

Figure 1-19   Watching the Float

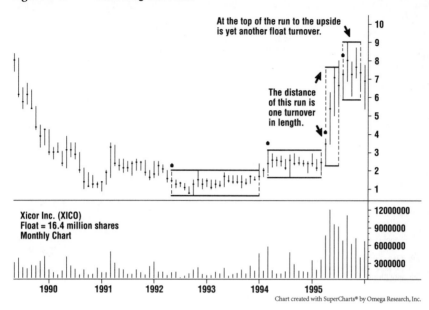

At the top of the run to the upside is yet another float turnover.

The distance of this run is one turnover in length.

Xicor Inc. (XICO)
Float = 16.4 million shares
Monthly Chart

Figure 1-20   Four Common Formations in Float Analysis

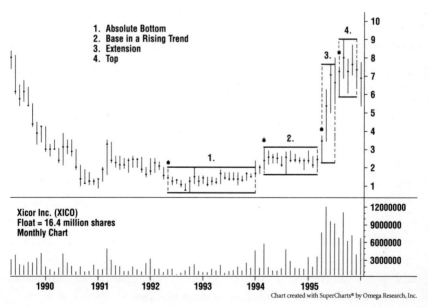

1. Absolute Bottom
2. Base in a Rising Trend
3. Extension
4. Top

Xicor Inc. (XICO)
Float = 16.4 million shares
Monthly Chart

Figure 1-21　　**Understanding Float Channel Lines**

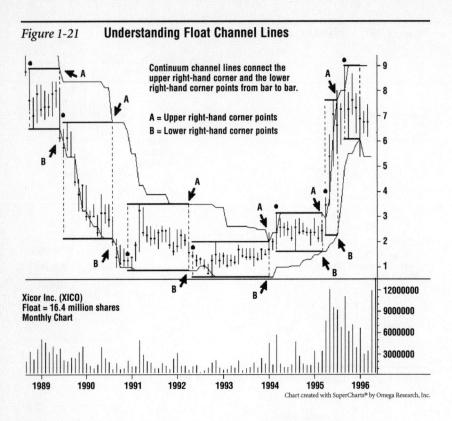

Continuum channel lines connect the upper right-hand corner and the lower right-hand corner points from bar to bar.

A = Upper right-hand corner points
B = Lower right-hand corner points

Xicor Inc. (XICO)
Float = 16.4 million shares
Monthly Chart

12000000
9000000
6000000
3000000

1989　1990　1991　1992　1993　1994　1995　1996

Chart created with SuperCharts® by Omega Research, Inc.

The Float Turnover as Seen with Channel Lines

Another way to view the turnover of Xicor's float historically is with cumulative-volume float channel lines. This approach lets us see the breakout buy
points more easily. In addition as we shall see in Chapter Four, these lines
give new meaning to what is known as support and resistance. To create
these lines, think of the float turnover as those rectangular boxes that were
plotted at different points on Xicor's chart. Now instead of plotting the whole
box, we will just plot the bar at the far right of the box. In other words, we'll
plot that part of the top horizontal line that is in the uppermost right-hand
corner and that part of the bottom line that is just in the lowest right-hand
corner. The actual monthly price bars with their high, low, and closing price
lines are left untouched. Thus, if we plot only these upper right (topmost)
and lower right (bottommost) parts of the upper and lower horizontal lines
on every bar, we create continuum, or channel, lines.

Figure 1-22   **Float Channel Lines**

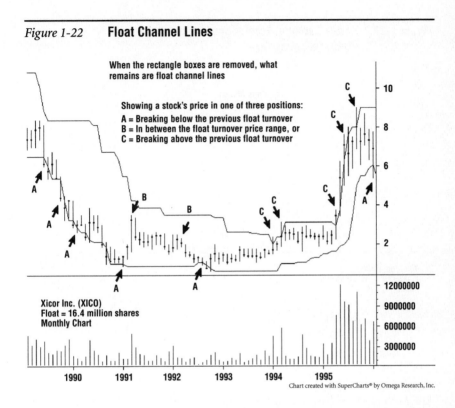

When the rectangle boxes are removed, what
remains are float channel lines

Showing a stock's price in one of three positions:
A = Breaking below the previous float turnover
B = In between the float turnover price range, or
C = Breaking above the previous float turnover

Xicor Inc. (XICO)
Float = 16.4 million shares
Monthly Chart

Chart created with SuperCharts® by Omega Research, Inc.

To better understand this process, look at figures 1-21 and 1-22. In figure 1-21, I have plotted the continuum, or channel, lines together with many of the rectangular float turnover boxes. Study this closely and you will see the relationship between the boxes and channel lines. Remember that the horizontal top and bottom lines serve as triggers to alert us when the price is dropping above or below an existing float turnover price range. Thus, prices at times will be shown dropping through the bottom right-hand corner of the rectangle or piercing above the upper right-hand corner. In effect, the continuum lines plot the float turnover's high and low price range on a bar-to-bar basis without showing the time component.

These continuum bars allow us to quickly identify where and when a stock's price has risen above or dropped below an existing float turnover. At any point in time, the price is trading either above, below, or within the most recently created float turnover (see figure 1-22).

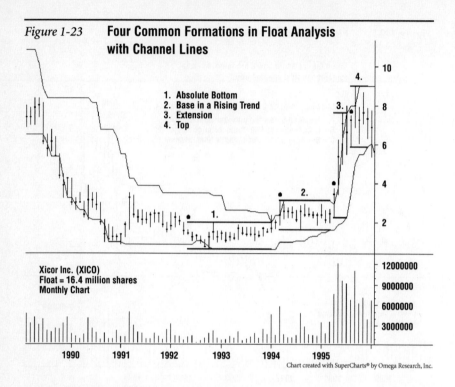

Figure 1-23 **Four Common Formations in Float Analysis with Channel Lines**

1. Absolute Bottom
2. Base in a Rising Trend
3. Extension
4. Top

Xicor Inc. (XICO)
Float = 16.4 million shares
Monthly Chart

Chart created with SuperCharts® by Omega Research, Inc.

The *float channel lines* are invaluable tools to study a stock's float turnover history. Using these lines we can see when the price rises above or falls below the float turnover range. This means that we can observe where the lowest float turnover at an absolute bottom or the uppermost float turnover at an absolute top occurs. Looking again at Xicor, we can combine our two methods for observing the float turnovers and once again see the float turnover formations in the context of the channel lines (see figure 1-23).

We have now seen four of the most common float turnover formations found in float analysis. They are:

    1. The Absolute Bottom
    2. The Base in a Rising Trend
    3. The Extension
    4. The Top[9]

---

9 This particular top turned out to be an intermediate top with the absolute top occurring a year later.

These float turnover formations are more than just fascinating lines on this particular stock chart. It is my contention that these and other related formations, which will be discussed in chapter 2, are commonplace and can be found on any stock's price and volume chart. To demonstrate this, let's look at a simple experiment with a random stock sample.

A Simple Random Sample Experiment

I need to say at the outset that this experiment is not an exacting, exhaustive, hard science enterprise, and I am not a research scientist. Float analysis has the potential to be hard science, but the lack of an exact historical database causes it to be far from precise. But it's a beginning, a science in its infancy. I am hoping that this book and experiment will help stimulate interest in float analysis so that such a database might be created.

As a background to understanding the experiment, you should know that I rely heavily for float numbers on a financial publication known as *Daily Graphs*. I have bought *Daily Graphs* chart books for years because they include a stock's float number and are a good source for finding winning stocks. The test I devised was to start at a random page of my most recent copy of *Daily Graphs* and look at the first 25 stocks I could find. I felt that 25 was a big enough number for my "keep-it-simple" purposes and would serve as a reasonably valid sample.

I looked for only bottom and top float turnover formations to see how many turned up. It should be noted that I did not choose a past issue of *Daily Graphs* in which I could get the results I wanted. I chose the most recent issue that I had at the time of this writing. I didn't know for sure what the results would be. I had confidence from years of experience that a large number of float turnover formations would appear. The *Daily Graphs* issue I chose was dated "Week Ending April 30, 1999," and I began on page 50 (see table 1.1).

As I analyzed the first 25 stocks, I realized that the experiment would not be fair unless one category of stock was eliminated. These were stocks that did not have enough volume trading data. They hadn't traded long enough for any float turnover formations to be detectable by the software. The software that Jan Arps and I invented to make float analysis possible requires at least enough cumulative volume to create two float turnovers before it can begin to make its observations. Initial public offerings (IPOs) are the best example of this eliminated category as well as stocks that don't have enough long-term trading volume to show even one float turnover. In the end, I had to search through 36 stocks and eliminate 11 to make up my list. As I mentioned at the beginning of this section, float analysis faces the difficulty of getting accurate historical data with which to do back testing, and this was made clear in this experiment. The float number found in the current issue of *Daily Graphs* may vary from the number that was reported in a previous issue, because float numbers can and do change.

Let's say XYZ Company issues 10 million outstanding shares. Of these 10 million, the management is holding 1.5 million. That makes the float at the time of the IPO 8.5 million. It stays at 8.5 million for six months, and then the management sells 200,000 shares. Now the float is 8.7 million. After another six months, management sells 600,000 shares. Now the float is 9.3 million. There is presently no database that keeps a record of these changes that can be downloaded into our software. The changes must be painstakingly recorded by looking through past issues of *Daily Graphs*. If you're attempting to evaluate a large number of stocks, these changes make for a time-consuming task. Now you know why I chose only 25 stocks for the experiment!

Thus, no experiment can be completely accurate. What I have done is used the best possible and available float numbers to make my calculations. I attempted to find the float numbers in previous issues for all 25 stocks that would make the results as accurate as possible. If no past issues could be found, I simply took the float number listed in the issue used for the experiment. At the end of this chapter, all 25 charts of the experiment are displayed (see table 1.1).

Table 1.1: Results of a Random Sample Experiment of 25 Stocks

	BOTTOM FORMATIONS	TOP FORMATIONS
1. Cam Data System (CADA)	2	0
2. Cambridge Technology (CATP)	1	2
3. Canandaigua Brands (CBRNA)	1	1
4. Candela Corp. (CLZR)	1	1
Career Education (CECO)	Eliminated (insufficient data)	
5. Carreker Antinori Inc. (CANI)	1	0
Carrier Access Corp. (CACS)	Eliminated (insufficient data)	

	BOTTOM FORMATIONS	TOP FORMATIONS
6. Caseys General Stores (CASY)	1	0
7. Catalyst International Inc. (CLYS)	1	0
Catapult Communications (CATT)	Eliminated (insufficient data)	
Cathay Bancorp (CATY)	Eliminated (insufficient data)	
8. Catherine's Stores Corp. (CATH)	1	0
Catskill Financial Corp. (CATB)	Eliminated (insufficient data)	
Cavalry Bancorp Inc. (CAVB)	Eliminated (insufficient data)	
9. CDNOW Inc. (CDNW)	3	2
10. Centocor Inc. (CNTO)	0	0
11. Central Sprinkler (CNSP)	3	1
12. Century Communications (CTYA)	1	0
Ceres Group (CERG)	Eliminated (insufficient data)	
13. Chancellor Media Corp. (AMFM)	1	1
14. Charter One Financial (COFI)	0	0
15. Chattem Inc. (CHTT)	1	0
Cheap Tickets (CTIX)	Eliminated (insufficient data)	
16. Check Point Software (CHKP)	1	2
17. Checkfree Holdings Corp. (CKFR)	1	0
18. Cheesecake Factory Inc. (CAKE)	1	1
19. Chico's FAS Inc. (CHCS)	1	0
Children's Place Retail (PLCE)	Eliminated (insufficient data)	
20. Chirex Inc. (CHRX)	1	0
21. Chiron Corp. (CHIR)	0	1
22. Ciena Corp. (CIEN)	1	1
Cinar Corporation (CINR)	Eliminated (insufficient data)	
23. Cintas Corp. (CTAS)	0	0
24. Cisco Systems (CSCO)	0	0
Citadel Communications (CITC)	Eliminated (insufficient data)	
25. Citizens Banking Corp. Mich. (CBCF)	0	0
TOTALS	**24**	**13**

Information found in *Daily Graphs*, April 30, 1999: 50.

Findings

Twenty-five stocks produced a total of 37 formations: 24 bottoms and 13 tops. Twenty out of 25 stocks, or 80%, had one or more top or bottom formations. Five out of 25 stocks, or 20%, had no top or bottom formations. Four of the five were in long-term *up-trends*. One stock had a multiple turnover formation.

Analyzing the Results

There are several points to be made from these results. First is to note that only 20% of the sample did not have a top or bottom float turnover formation of any kind. Thus, 80% had at least one float turnover formation, and several had two or more. These formations are commonplace.

> Only 20% of the sample did not have a top or bottom float turnover formation of any kind. Thus, 80% had at least one float turnover formation, and several had two or more. These formations are commonplace.

In addition, if we take a close look at the five stocks that have no top or bottom float turnover formations, Centocor, Charter One Financial, Cintas Corp., Cisco Systems, and Citizens Banking Corp., we find that four of these, Charter One Financial, Cintas Corp., Cisco Systems, and Citizens Banking Corp., are in long-term up-trends and as yet have not made a top. At some point in the future they will. The one remaining stock, Centocor, is a special case that is making what I call a multiple turnover formation. It has been going sideways for years and has formed over seven float turnovers in the process. Some of these float turnovers could be considered bottoms or tops, but instead I chose to list it as zero. In later chapters, I will discuss these multiple turnover stocks in greater detail because they are potentially very powerful stocks.

It should also be noted that there are a greater number of bottom formations than top formations. I suspect that this occurs because we're looking at stocks of the 1990s when we have had the greatest bull market in history. Thus, it makes sense that there are fewer stocks making tops and more stocks rising from bottom formations.

A Question for You

Study the charts at the end of this chapter and ask yourself, what is the basic principle of float analysis? I know what I believe! It is simply that a stock trades in relation to its float. This may seem obvious, but traditional technical analysis before float analysis did not incorporate the float into price and volume charts. When you see a price and volume chart, you are only looking at two-thirds of the total picture. The missing third is the shares actually available for trading. Because float analysis shows these tradable shares, it represents a new, holistic approach to stock analysis. The float should be seen as an equal partner with price and volume. You can't look at three similar charts and think that because they look the same, the companies are exactly alike. The difference is in the floating supply of shares. You can't truly understand the type of stock you're buying unless the float is included in the discussion.

> The basic principle of float analysis is simply — a stock trades in relation to its float. The float turnover formations show a direct relationship between past trading volume and a stock's future price direction.

In Closing

The ideas in this and upcoming chapters should be of great interest to market technicians. These ideas can forever change the way technicians look at price and volume charts. This is because float turnover formations show a direct relationship between past trading volume and a stock's future price direction. They help to clarify when a stock's price has a sound base of support underneath it or when it has a weak ceiling of resistance above it. They create new, measurable definitions of bottoms and tops. They are invaluable tools to better analyze price and volume charts. But most importantly, **float analysis will make people money** by helping them in their timing of stock purchases and sales. I know this to be a fact because in the 16 months from September 1998 to January 2000, I made a tenfold move with the money in my portfolio.

Note that in the time frame that I traded my money to make a tenfold move, the stock market was in a new bull phase, a great time to be into stocks. I should also state that I have been intensely studying the stock market for

Float turnover formations are invaluable tools to better analyze price and volume charts. But most importantly, float analysis will make people money by helping them in their timing of stock purchases and sales.

some time. I am a student of William O'Neil, the founder of *Investor's Business Daily*. His ideas have had a profound impact on my methods. Using his techniques, I have learned how to spot broad market bottoms and the new leading stocks coming out of these corrective *bear market* conditions. I should also point out that during my eight years of trading, I have had plenty of losing trades. In addition, the reader should know that I do not rely **only** on float analysis to decide when to buy or sell a stock. It is my primary tool, and I would not trade without it, but I also use *fundamental analysis*. In addition, I read *Investor's Business Daily* every day; it's the best paper in the business for technicians like myself.

Figure 1-24 **The 25 Stocks in a Simple Random Sample Test— Cam Data System (CADA)**

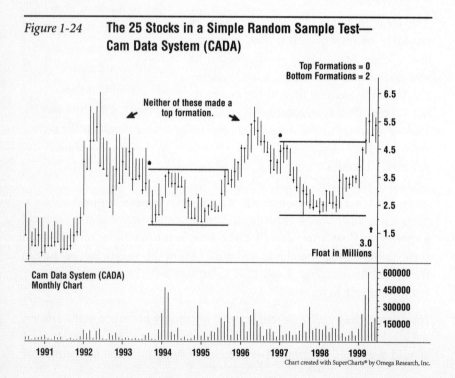

Chart created with SuperCharts® by Omega Research, Inc.

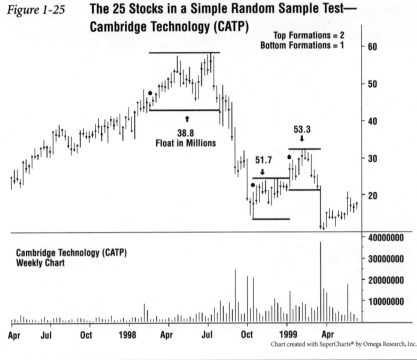

Figure 1-25   The 25 Stocks in a Simple Random Sample Test—
Cambridge Technology (CATP)

Top Formations = 2
Bottom Formations = 1

38.8
Float in Millions

51.7
↓

53.3
↓

Cambridge Technology (CATP)
Weekly Chart

Chart created with SuperCharts® by Omega Research, Inc.

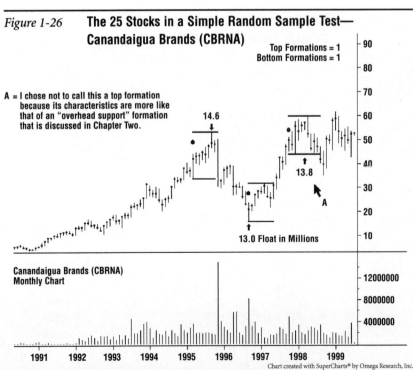

Figure 1-26   The 25 Stocks in a Simple Random Sample Test—
Canandaigua Brands (CBRNA)

Top Formations = 1
Bottom Formations = 1

A = I chose not to call this a top formation
because its characteristics are more like
that of an "overhead support" formation
that is discussed in Chapter Two.

14.6
↓

13.8
↑

A

13.0 Float in Millions

Canandaigua Brands (CBRNA)
Monthly Chart

Chart created with SuperCharts® by Omega Research, Inc.

Figure 1-27 **The 25 Stocks in a Simple Random Sample Test—Candela Corp. (CLZR)**

Top Formations = 1
Bottom Formations = 1

Float in Millions 3.2

Candela Corp. (CLZR)
Weekly Chart

Chart created with SuperCharts® by Omega Research, Inc.

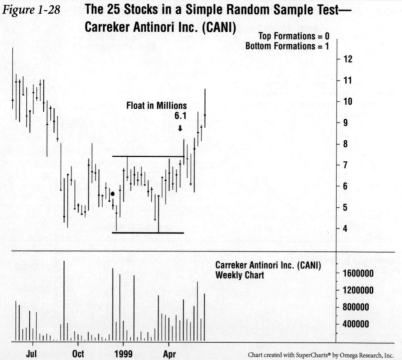

Figure 1-28 **The 25 Stocks in a Simple Random Sample Test— Carreker Antinori Inc. (CANI)**

Top Formations = 0
Bottom Formations = 1

Float in Millions
6.1

Carreker Antinori Inc. (CANI)
Weekly Chart

Chart created with SuperCharts® by Omega Research, Inc.

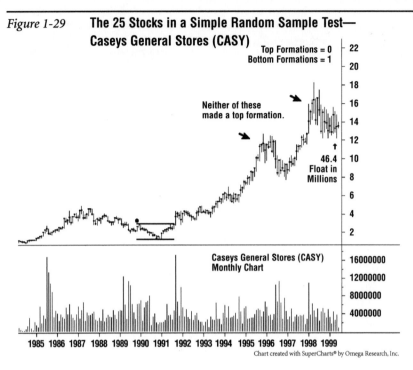

Figure 1-29   **The 25 Stocks in a Simple Random Sample Test—Caseys General Stores (CASY)**

Top Formations = 0
Bottom Formations = 1

Neither of these made a top formation.

46.4 Float in Millions

Caseys General Stores (CASY) Monthly Chart

Chart created with SuperCharts® by Omega Research, Inc.

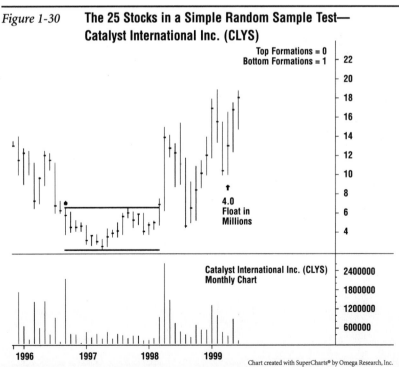

Figure 1-30   **The 25 Stocks in a Simple Random Sample Test—Catalyst International Inc. (CLYS)**

Top Formations = 0
Bottom Formations = 1

4.0 Float in Millions

Catalyst International Inc. (CLYS) Monthly Chart

Chart created with SuperCharts® by Omega Research, Inc.

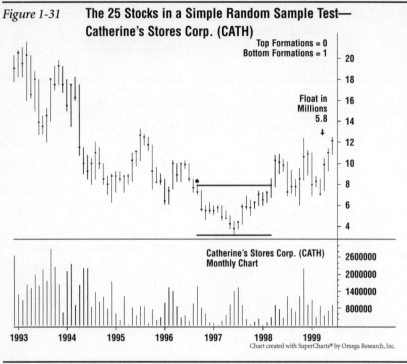

Figure 1-31   **The 25 Stocks in a Simple Random Sample Test— Catherine's Stores Corp. (CATH)**

Top Formations = 0
Bottom Formations = 1

Float in
Millions
5.8
↓

Catherine's Stores Corp. (CATH)
Monthly Chart

Chart created with SuperCharts® by Omega Research, Inc.

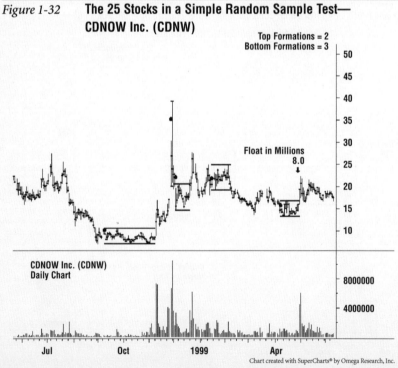

Figure 1-32   **The 25 Stocks in a Simple Random Sample Test— CDNOW Inc. (CDNW)**

Top Formations = 2
Bottom Formations = 3

Float in Millions
8.0
↓

CDNOW Inc. (CDNW)
Daily Chart

Chart created with SuperCharts® by Omega Research, Inc.

Figure 1-33 The 25 Stocks in a Simple Random Sample Test— Centocor Inc. (CNTO)

Top Formations = 0
Bottom Formations = 0

This is a special type of stock that is making what I call a "multiple turnover" formation. It has been going sideways for years with at least seven float turnovers.

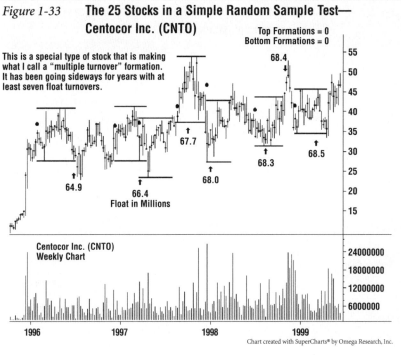

Centocor Inc. (CNTO)
Weekly Chart

Figure 1-34 The 25 Stocks in a Simple Random Sample Test— Central Sprinkler (CNSP)

Top Formations = 1
Bottom Formations = 3

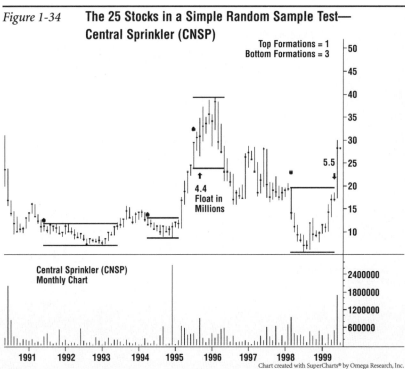

Central Sprinkler (CNSP)
Monthly Chart

Chart created with SuperCharts® by Omega Research, Inc.

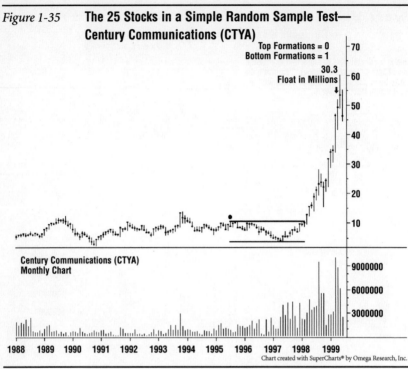

Figure 1-35 **The 25 Stocks in a Simple Random Sample Test—Century Communications (CTYA)**

Top Formations = 0
Bottom Formations = 1

30.3
Float in Millions

Century Communications (CTYA)
Monthly Chart

1988 1989 1990 1991 1992 1993 1994 1995 1996 1997 1998 1999

Chart created with SuperCharts® by Omega Research, Inc.

Figure 1-36 **The 25 Stocks in a Simple Random Sample Test—Chancellor Media Corp. (AMFM)**

Top Formations = 1
Bottom Formations = 1

61.8
Float in
Millions

Chancellor Media Corp. (AMFM)
Weekly Chart

1997 1998 1999

Chart created with SuperCharts® by Omega Research, Inc.

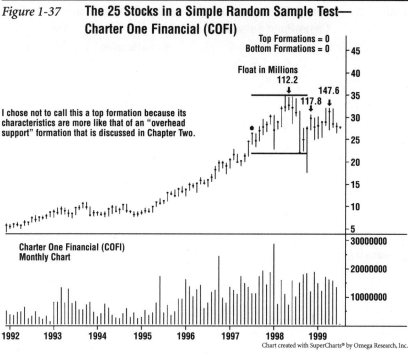

Figure 1-37 **The 25 Stocks in a Simple Random Sample Test—Charter One Financial (COFI)**

Top Formations = 0
Bottom Formations = 0

Float in Millions
112.2

147.6
117.8

I chose not to call this a top formation because its characteristics are more like that of an "overhead support" formation that is discussed in Chapter Two.

Charter One Financial (COFI)
Monthly Chart

Chart created with SuperCharts® by Omega Research, Inc.

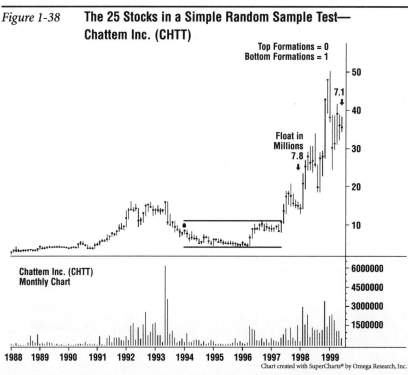

Figure 1-38 **The 25 Stocks in a Simple Random Sample Test—Chattem Inc. (CHTT)**

Top Formations = 0
Bottom Formations = 1

7.1

Float in
Millions
7.8

Chattem Inc. (CHTT)
Monthly Chart

Chart created with SuperCharts® by Omega Research, Inc.

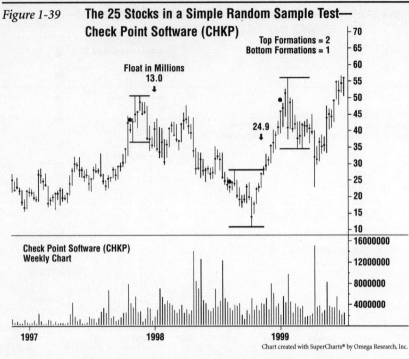

Figure 1-39   The 25 Stocks in a Simple Random Sample Test—
Check Point Software (CHKP)

Top Formations = 2
Bottom Formations = 1

Float in Millions
13.0

24.9

Check Point Software (CHKP)
Weekly Chart

Chart created with SuperCharts® by Omega Research, Inc.

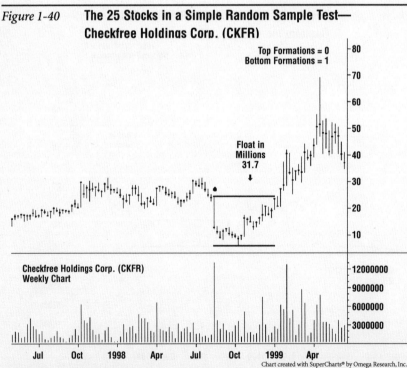

Figure 1-40   The 25 Stocks in a Simple Random Sample Test—
Checkfree Holdings Corp. (CKFR)

Top Formations = 0
Bottom Formations = 1

Float in
Millions
31.7

Checkfree Holdings Corp. (CKFR)
Weekly Chart

Chart created with SuperCharts® by Omega Research, Inc.

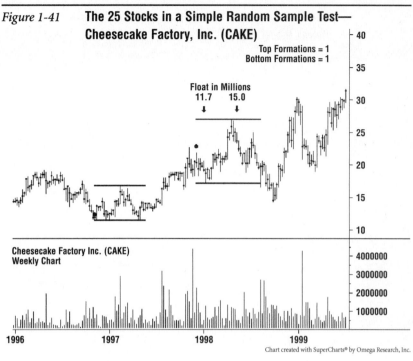

Figure 1-41 **The 25 Stocks in a Simple Random Sample Test—
Cheesecake Factory, Inc. (CAKE)**

Top Formations = 1
Bottom Formations = 1

Float in Millions
11.7   15.0

Cheesecake Factory Inc. (CAKE)
Weekly Chart

Chart created with SuperCharts® by Omega Research, Inc.

Figure 1-42 **The 25 Stocks in a Simple Random Sample Test—
Chico's FAS, Inc. (CHCS)**

Top Formations = 0
Bottom Formations = 1

6.1

Float in
Millions
5.8

Chico's FAS, Inc. (CHCS)
Weekly Chart

Chart created with SuperCharts® by Omega Research, Inc.

Figure 1-43 **The 25 Stocks in a Simple Random Sample Test—Chirex Inc. (CHRX)**

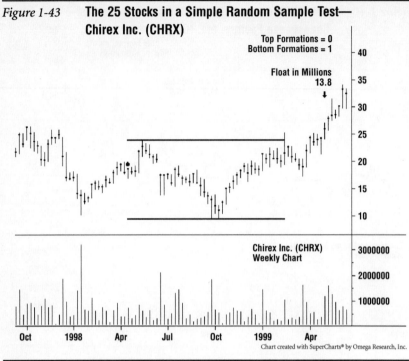

Top Formations = 0
Bottom Formations = 1

Float in Millions
13.8

Chirex Inc. (CHRX)
Weekly Chart

Chart created with SuperCharts® by Omega Research, Inc.

Figure 1-44 **The 25 Stocks in a Simple Random Sample Test—Chiron Corp. (CHIR)**

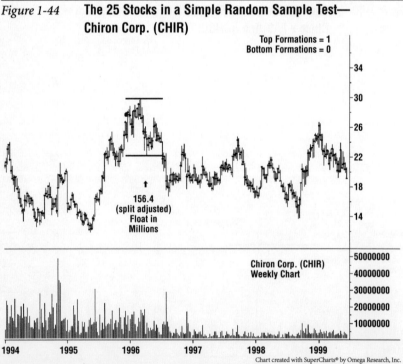

Top Formations = 1
Bottom Formations = 0

156.4
(split adjusted)
Float in
Millions

Chiron Corp. (CHIR)
Weekly Chart

Chart created with SuperCharts® by Omega Research, Inc.

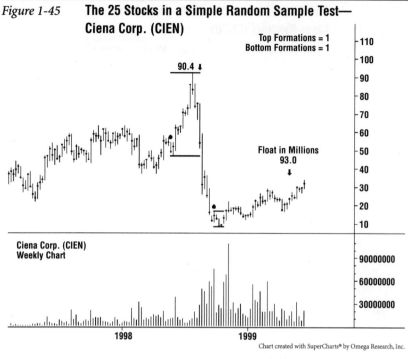

Figure 1-45 **The 25 Stocks in a Simple Random Sample Test—
Ciena Corp. (CIEN)**

Top Formations = 1
Bottom Formations = 1

90.4 ↓

Float in Millions
93.0
↓

Ciena Corp. (CIEN)
Weekly Chart

1998   1999

Chart created with SuperCharts® by Omega Research, Inc.

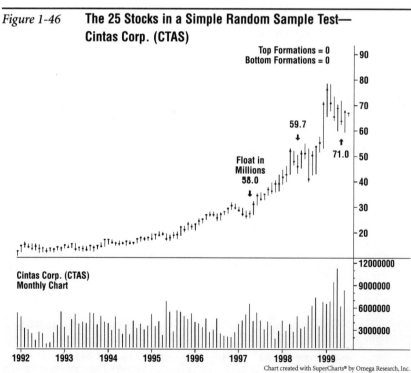

Figure 1-46 **The 25 Stocks in a Simple Random Sample Test—
Cintas Corp. (CTAS)**

Top Formations = 0
Bottom Formations = 0

59.7
↓

71.0 ↑

Float in
Millions
58.0
↓

Cintas Corp. (CTAS)
Monthly Chart

1992   1993   1994   1995   1996   1997   1998   1999

Chart created with SuperCharts® by Omega Research, Inc.

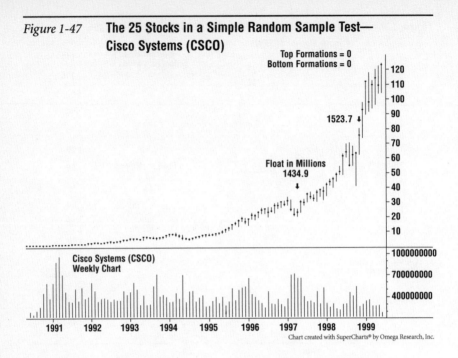

Figure 1-47   The 25 Stocks in a Simple Random Sample Test—
               Cisco Systems (CSCO)

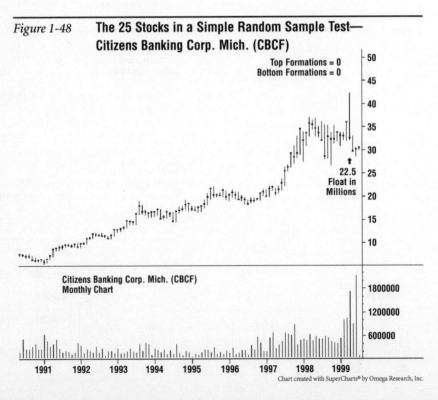

Figure 1-48   The 25 Stocks in a Simple Random Sample Test—
               Citizens Banking Corp. Mich. (CBCF)

CHAPTER TWO

Ten Breakthrough Discoveries

That Will Change the Way You Analyze Stock Charts

. . . for what he had discovered was a New World.

B ecause it is my contention that float turnover formations are commonplace and until now undocumented, they can be described as discoveries. In my research, I have made 10 discoveries. These discoveries are the foundation for a float analysis model of price and volume behavior.

Each discovery will be presented with corresponding formations as well as breakout trading points. For each of the formations there are several examples. Appendix A is a compendium of examples from all the categories for reference and research purposes.

The 10 Discoveries

1 Multiple float turnover formations are the strongest bases of support.

2 Single float turnover formations with a breakout buy point always occur at absolute bottoms and are also found at intermediate bottoms.

3 Single float turnover formations with a breakout sell point always occur at absolute tops and are also found at intermediate tops.

4 Single float turnover formations with a breakout buy point occur at the bottom of price corrections.

5 Single float turnover formations with a breakout buy point occur at price consolidation basing areas in up-trends.

6 Price support in up-trends occurs as a stock's price falls below the float turnover price range, thus giving rise to a single float turnover *overhead support formation* with a breakout to the downside buy point.

7 Single float turnover formations with a sell point occur in *price extensions* both slow and fast.

8 Price support in up-trends commonly occurs as a stock's price falls to the 50% point in the float turnover price range, giving rise to *upright flag formations* with a buy point.

9 Price resistance in *down-trends* occurs as a stock's price rises to the 50% point in the float turnover price range, giving rise to *inverted flag formations* with a sell point.

10 Price resistance in down-trends following a topping formation occurs as a stock's price rises above the float turnover price range, thus giving rise to *weak bases of support* with a breakout to the upside sell point.

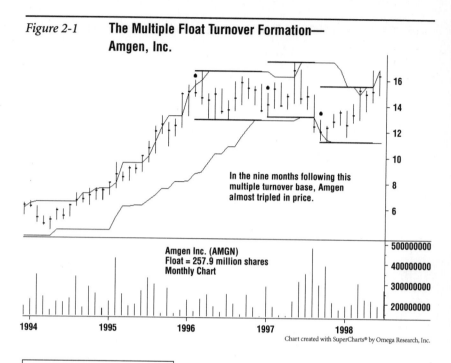

Figure 2-1   **The Multiple Float Turnover Formation— Amgen, Inc.**

In the nine months following this multiple turnover base, Amgen almost tripled in price.

Amgen Inc. (AMGN)
Float = 257.9 million shares
Monthly Chart

Chart created with SuperCharts® by Omega Research, Inc.

Discovery 1	The Multiple Float Turnover Formation
Multiple float turnover formations are the strongest bases of support.	

When a stock is seen moving in a long sideways price pattern, it is common to see multiple float turnovers. These formations are the strongest of the strong and represent fantastic buying opportunities when the price breaks into *new high ground*.

During these extended sideways moves, the price appears to be unable to make any headway. At times, it will appear to have made a final top. This is probably occurring because the fundamental value of the company at the present level is in question or the stock's price has come "too far, too fast" and needs a corrective base-building "pause to refresh." Accumulation during this formation is gradual, but when the breakout to the upside comes, the move is usually quite large. Amgen (AMGN), Yahoo! (YHOO), and Netb@nk (NTBK) are good examples of these formations (see figures 2-1, 2-2, and 2-3).

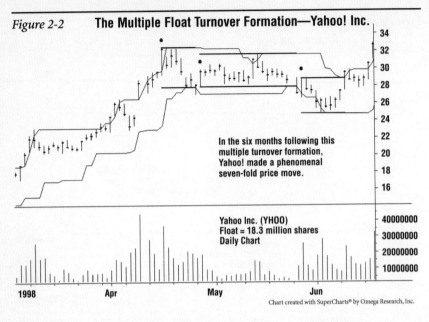

Figure 2-2   **The Multiple Float Turnover Formation—Yahoo! Inc.**

In the six months following this multiple turnover formation, Yahoo! made a phenomenal seven-fold price move.

Yahoo Inc. (YHOO)
Float = 18.3 million shares
Daily Chart

Chart created with SuperCharts® by Omega Research, Inc.

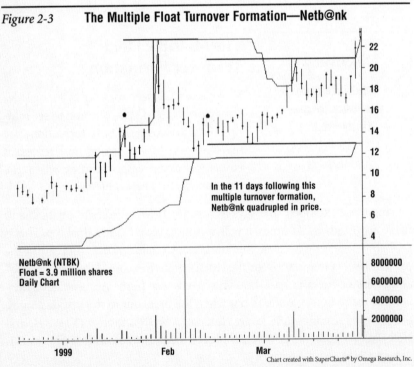

Figure 2-3   **The Multiple Float Turnover Formation—Netb@nk**

In the 11 days following this multiple turnover formation, Netb@nk quadrupled in price.

Netb@nk (NTBK)
Float = 3.9 million shares
Daily Chart

Chart created with SuperCharts® by Omega Research, Inc.

Discoveries 2 and 3

Single float turnover formations with a breakout buy point always occur at absolute bottoms and are also found at intermediate bottoms.

Single float turnover formations with a breakout sell point always occur at absolute tops and are also found at intermediate tops.

The Bottom Formation and the Top Formation

Bottoms and tops are the most common of all float analysis formations. Stocks just don't go public and then go up or down forever. At some point, the stock's price is going to change direction. Wherever a stock has had a long price decline and then a subsequent rise in price, you'll find a float turnover bottom formation. Wherever a stock has had a long price rise and then a subsequent decline, you'll find a float turnover top formation.

Figure 2-4 **Bottom and Top Formations**

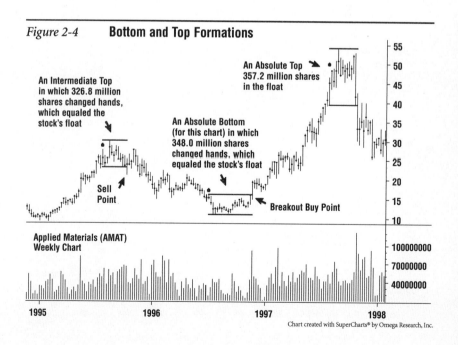

Chart created with SuperCharts® by Omega Research, Inc.

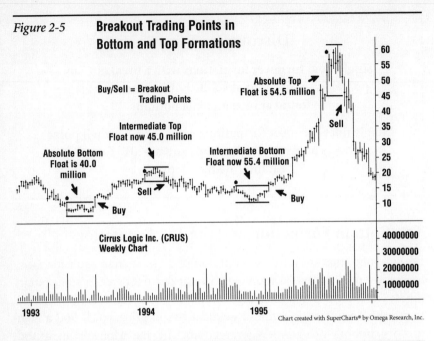

Figure 2-5   **Breakout Trading Points in Bottom and Top Formations**

Buy/Sell = Breakout Trading Points

Absolute Top
Float is 54.5 million

Sell

Intermediate Top
Float now 45.0 million

Intermediate Bottom
Float now 55.4 million

Absolute Bottom
Float is 40.0 million

Sell

Buy

Buy

Cirrus Logic Inc. (CRUS)
Weekly Chart

Chart created with SuperCharts® by Omega Research, Inc.

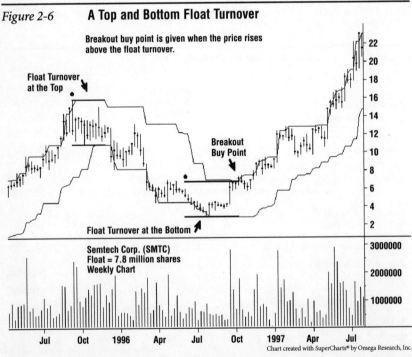

Figure 2-6   **A Top and Bottom Float Turnover**

Breakout buy point is given when the price rises above the float turnover.

Float Turnover at the Top

Breakout Buy Point

Float Turnover at the Bottom

Semtech Corp. (SMTC)
Float = 7.8 million shares
Weekly Chart

Chart created with SuperCharts® by Omega Research, Inc.

Bottom and top formations are so common that they can often be seen on the very same chart. This is especially true on stocks that are volatile with wide swings in prices. Three examples that demonstrate this are Applied Materials (AMAT), Cirrus Logic (CRUS), and Semtech Corp. (SMTC) (see figures 2-4, 2-5, and 2-6). The breakout buy point in a bottom formation is where the price rises above the float. The breakout sell point for top formations is where the price declines below the float.

Discovery 4

Single float turnover formations with a breakout buy point occur at the bottom of price corrections.

The Base of Support within a Correction Formation

Stocks that are in strong up-trends often pause and go down in price for a while before heading back up into new high ground. This downturn in price can last days, weeks, or months and is called a *correction*. In this formation, the number of shares that trades hands at the bottom of the correction equals the number of shares in the float.

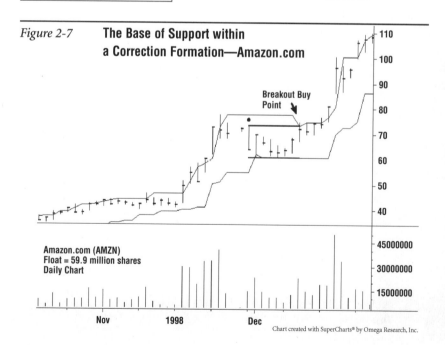

Figure 2-7   **The Base of Support within a Correction Formation—Amazon.com**

Breakout Buy Point

Amazon.com (AMZN)
Float = 59.9 million shares
Daily Chart

Nov   1998   Dec

Chart created with SuperCharts® by Omega Research, Inc.

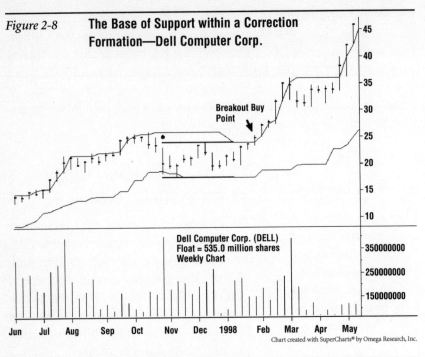

Figure 2-8   **The Base of Support within a Correction Formation—Dell Computer Corp.**

Breakout Buy Point

Dell Computer Corp. (DELL)
Float = 535.0 million shares
Weekly Chart

Chart created with SuperCharts® by Omega Research, Inc.

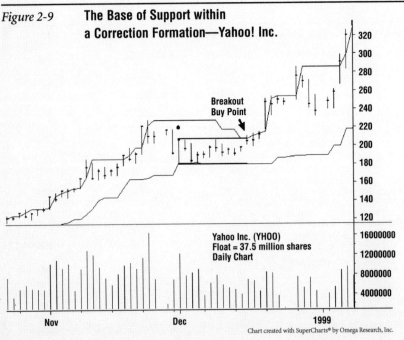

Figure 2-9   **The Base of Support within a Correction Formation—Yahoo! Inc.**

Breakout Buy Point

Yahoo Inc. (YHOO)
Float = 37.5 million shares
Daily Chart

Chart created with SuperCharts® by Omega Research, Inc.

The breakout buy point here is again where the price rises above the float turnover range. Several good examples include Amazon.com (AMZN), Dell Computer Corp. (DELL), and Yahoo! (YHOO) (see figures 2-7, 2-8, and 2-9). In each case, a float turnover occurred right at the bottom of a correction.

Discovery 5

Single float turnover formations with a breakout buy point occur at price consolidation basing areas in up-trends.

The Strong Sideways Base of Support in an Up-Trend Formation

Stocks that are in strong price up-trends will often have a sideways consolidation price move before heading back up into new high ground. This sideways price move is often referred to as basing activity. In this formation, while the stock's price is moving sideways, the number of shares that trades hands equals one float turnover.

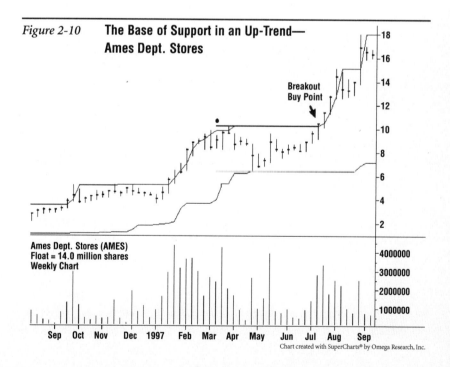

Figure 2-10   **The Base of Support in an Up-Trend— Ames Dept. Stores**

Breakout Buy Point

Ames Dept. Stores (AMES)
Float = 14.0 million shares
Weekly Chart

Chart created with SuperCharts® by Omega Research, Inc.

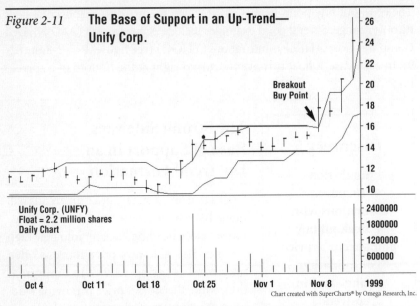

Figure 2-11 **The Base of Support in an Up-Trend—
Unify Corp.**

Breakout
Buy Point

Unify Corp. (UNFY)
Float = 2.2 million shares
Daily Chart

26
24
22
20
18
16
14
12
10

2400000
1800000
1200000
600000

Oct 4   Oct 11   Oct 18   Oct 25   Nov 1   Nov 8   1999

Chart created with SuperCharts® by Omega Research, Inc.

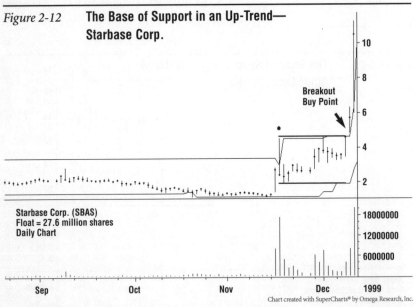

Figure 2-12 **The Base of Support in an Up-Trend—
Starbase Corp.**

Breakout
Buy Point

Starbase Corp. (SBAS)
Float = 27.6 million shares
Daily Chart

10
8
6
4
2

18000000
12000000
6000000

Sep   Oct   Nov   Dec   1999

Chart created with SuperCharts® by Omega Research, Inc.

The investors who buy in the sideways move create a base of support upon which the price may rise higher. A breakout buy point occurs just as the price rises above the float turnover once the number of shares traded in the consolidation area equals the float. Three examples of the sideways base are Ames Dept. Stores (AMES), Unify Corp. (UNFY), and Starbase Corp. (SBAS) (see figures 2-10, 2-11, and 2-12).

Discovery 6

Price support in up-trends occurs as a stock's price falls below the float turnover price range, thus giving rise to a single float turnover "overhead support" formation with a breakout to the downside buy point.

The Overhead Base of Support Formation

The overhead base of support formation is one of the most fascinating in float analysis. Here, as in the previous formation, a stock in a price up-trend has a sideways consolidation basing price move before heading into new high ground. The only difference between this formation and the previous one is that, when the turnover is complete, the price drops just below the float turnover before beginning to rise in price.

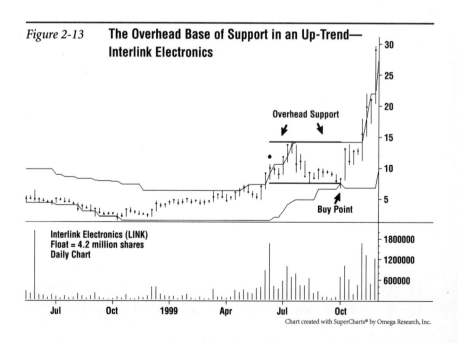

Figure 2-13 **The Overhead Base of Support in an Up-Trend— Interlink Electronics**

Interlink Electronics (LINK)
Float = 4.2 million shares
Daily Chart

Chart created with SuperCharts® by Omega Research, Inc.

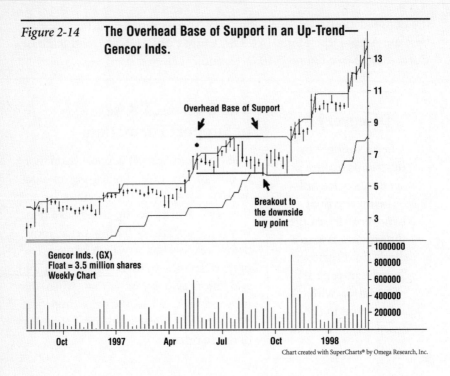

Figure 2-14 **The Overhead Base of Support in an Up-Trend— Gencor Inds.**

Overhead Base of Support

Breakout to the downside buy point

Gencor Inds. (GX)
Float = 3.5 million shares
Weekly Chart

Chart created with SuperCharts® by Omega Research, Inc.

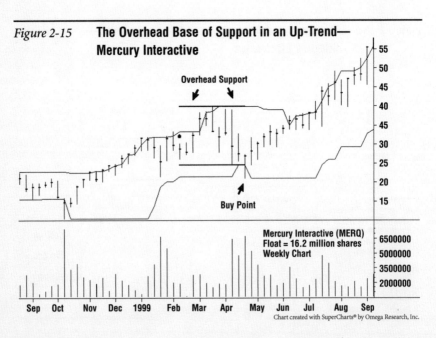

Figure 2-15 **The Overhead Base of Support in an Up-Trend— Mercury Interactive**

Overhead Support

Buy Point

Mercury Interactive (MERQ)
Float = 16.2 million shares
Weekly Chart

Chart created with SuperCharts® by Omega Research, Inc.

When the price is going sideways, the stock is being accumulated by investors who recognize its value. When the accumulation is complete and the entire float is being held tightly, the price tests this accumulation zone by briefly dropping below it. Because the ownership above the price at this point is strong and holding tight, the price abruptly reverses direction and begins to head higher. Examples of this are Interlink Electronics (LINK), Gencor Inds. (GX), and Mercury Interactive (MERQ) (see figures 2-13, 2-14, and 2-15).

Discovery 7

Single float turnover formations with a trading sell point occur in price extensions both slow and fast.

The Slow Extension Formation

Extension formations are also some of the most interesting in float analysis. They have powerful implications for deciding when to sell a stock and also when to short it. The term *price extension* refers here to the movement of a stock's price through one complete float turnover from a bottom to a top.

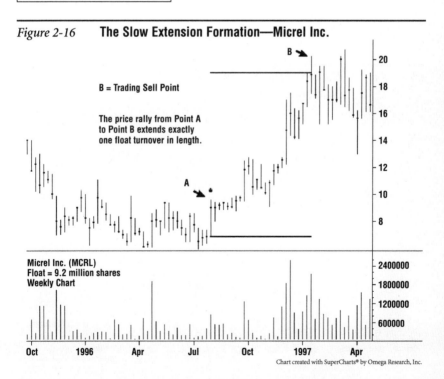

Figure 2-16 **The Slow Extension Formation—Micrel Inc.**

B = Trading Sell Point

The price rally from Point A to Point B extends exactly one float turnover in length.

Micrel Inc. (MCRL)
Float = 9.2 million shares
Weekly Chart

Chart created with SuperCharts® by Omega Research, Inc.

Figure 2-17 **The Slow Extension Formation—Petsmart Inc.**

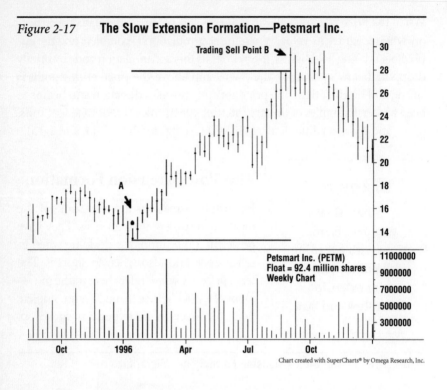

Trading Sell Point B

A

Petsmart Inc. (PETM)
Float = 92.4 million shares
Weekly Chart

Oct   1996   Apr   Jul   Oct

Chart created with SuperCharts® by Omega Research, Inc.

Figure 2-18 **The Slow Extension Formation—
Countrywide Credit**

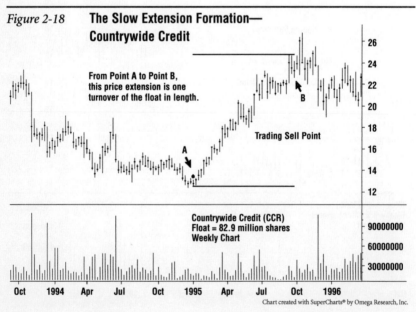

From Point A to Point B,
this price extension is one
turnover of the float in length.

B

Trading Sell Point

A

Countrywide Credit (CCR)
Float = 82.9 million shares
Weekly Chart

Oct   1994   Apr   Jul   Oct   1995   Apr   Jul   Oct   1996

Chart created with SuperCharts® by Omega Research, Inc.

Extension formations fall into two broad categories — slow and fast. Slow-moving extension formations are those that require months for the extension to form. The fast-moving formations occur in weeks or days. Three examples of slow-moving extension formations include Micrel (MCRL), Petsmart (PETM), and Countrywide Credit (CCR) (see figures 2-16, 2-17, and 2-18).

The Fast Extension Formation

On rare occasions, some stocks will make very fast runs to the upside. These moves are dramatic and exhilarating, particularly if one owns shares of these rocket stocks. Sometimes these price moves last exactly one float turnover. When the total number of shares in the float trades hands once, the stock's price reverses direction. In theory, this occurs because the owners at the lower price levels of the float turnover begin selling to the new owners at the top. The result is that the price corrects downward toward equilibrium at middle ground. To get a better sense of how these float turnover formations can change rapidly, it helps to see them in a sequence of charts. Two companies that had fast price moves to the upside are TSR (TSRI) and Zenith Electronics (ZE) (see figures 2-19, 2-20, 2-21, 2-22, 2-23, 2-24, and 2-25).

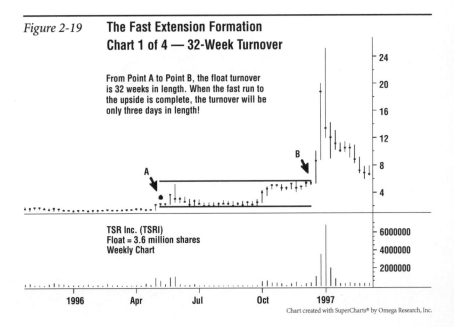

Figure 2-19 **The Fast Extension Formation
Chart 1 of 4 — 32-Week Turnover**

From Point A to Point B, the float turnover
is 32 weeks in length. When the fast run to
the upside is complete, the turnover will be
only three days in length!

TSR Inc. (TSRI)
Float = 3.6 million shares
Weekly Chart

Chart created with SuperCharts® by Omega Research, Inc.

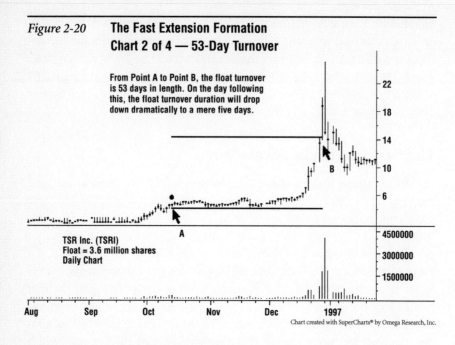

Figure 2-20 **The Fast Extension Formation
Chart 2 of 4 — 53-Day Turnover**

From Point A to Point B, the float turnover
is 53 days in length. On the day following
this, the float turnover duration will drop
down dramatically to a mere five days.

B

A

TSR Inc. (TSRI)
Float = 3.6 million shares
Daily Chart

Chart created with SuperCharts® by Omega Research, Inc.

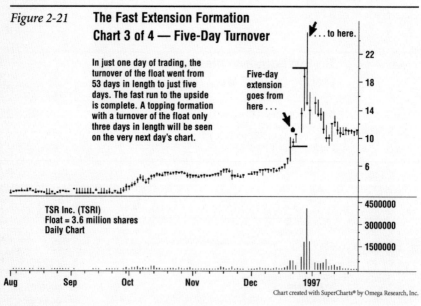

Figure 2-21 **The Fast Extension Formation
Chart 3 of 4 — Five-Day Turnover**

. . . to here.

In just one day of trading, the
turnover of the float went from
53 days in length to just five
days. The fast run to the upside
is complete. A topping formation
with a turnover of the float only
three days in length will be seen
on the very next day's chart.

Five-day
extension
goes from
here . . .

TSR Inc. (TSRI)
Float = 3.6 million shares
Daily Chart

Chart created with SuperCharts® by Omega Research, Inc.

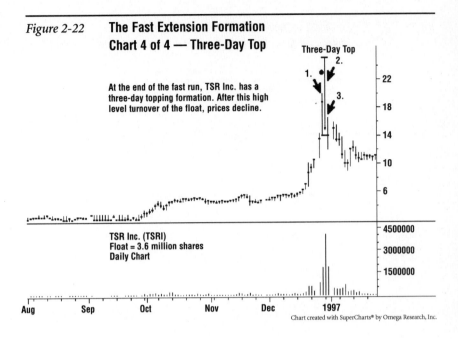

Figure 2-22 **The Fast Extension Formation**
Chart 4 of 4 — Three-Day Top

Three-Day Top

At the end of the fast run, TSR Inc. has a
three-day topping formation. After this high
level turnover of the float, prices decline.

TSR Inc. (TSRI)
Float = 3.6 million shares
Daily Chart

Chart created with SuperCharts® by Omega Research, Inc.

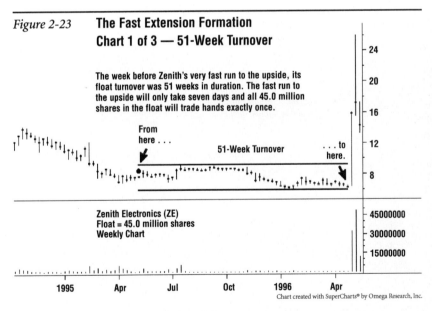

Figure 2-23 **The Fast Extension Formation**
Chart 1 of 3 — 51-Week Turnover

The week before Zenith's very fast run to the upside, its
float turnover was 51 weeks in duration. The fast run to
the upside will only take seven days and all 45.0 million
shares in the float will trade hands exactly once.

From
here . . .

51-Week Turnover

. . . to
here.

Zenith Electronics (ZE)
Float = 45.0 million shares
Weekly Chart

Chart created with SuperCharts® by Omega Research, Inc.

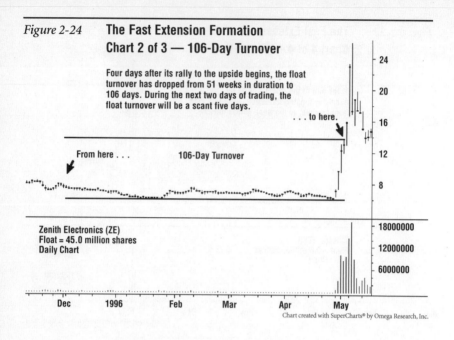

Figure 2-24   **The Fast Extension Formation
Chart 2 of 3 — 106-Day Turnover**

Four days after its rally to the upside begins, the float
turnover has dropped from 51 weeks in duration to
106 days. During the next two days of trading, the
float turnover will be a scant five days.

. . . to here.

From here . . .   106-Day Turnover

Zenith Electronics (ZE)
Float = 45.0 million shares
Daily Chart

Dec   1996   Feb   Mar   Apr   May

Chart created with SuperCharts® by Omega Research, Inc.

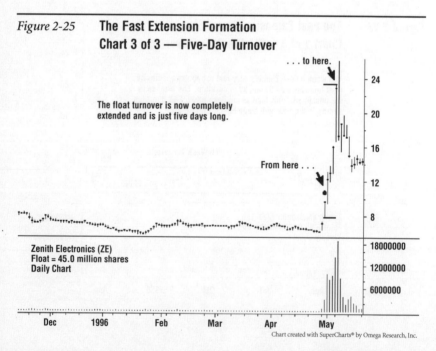

Figure 2-25   **The Fast Extension Formation
Chart 3 of 3 — Five-Day Turnover**

. . . to here.

The float turnover is now completely
extended and is just five days long.

From here . . .

Zenith Electronics (ZE)
Float = 45.0 million shares
Daily Chart

Dec   1996   Feb   Mar   Apr   May

Chart created with SuperCharts® by Omega Research, Inc.

<table>
<tr><td>

Discovery 8

Price support in up-trends commonly occurs as a stock's price falls to the 50% point in the float turnover price range, giving rise to upright flag formations with a buy point.

</td></tr>
</table>

The Upright Flag Formation

There are two distinct types of flag formations,[10] the *upright* and the *inverted*. The upright is found near bottoms and in up-trends. The inverted flag formation is found near tops and in down-trends.

Imagine a flag waving in the wind: the upright flag formation has a stock's price making a *fast move to the upside* that corresponds to the image of a flag pole. Then the price goes sideways or down to form a triangular pennant shape or a rectangular flag shape. These are highly profitable formations since the pennant or flag part of the formation is actually deriving support from the lower half of the flagpole. It's a case of the top half of the

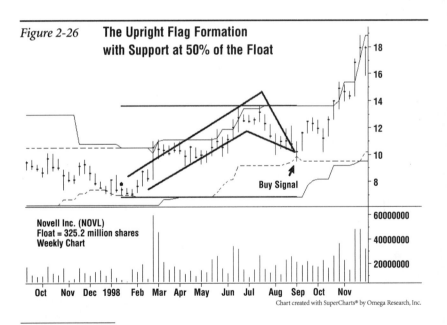

Figure 2-26   **The Upright Flag Formation with Support at 50% of the Float**

Buy Signal

Novell Inc. (NOVL)
Float = 325.2 million shares
Weekly Chart

Oct   Nov   Dec 1998 Feb   Mar   Apr   May   Jun   Jul   Aug   Sep   Oct   Nov

Chart created with SuperCharts® by Omega Research, Inc.

---

10 I use the term *flag formation* in its broadest possible sense. I call these formations *flags* because to me that is what they most closely resemble. Other technicians may disagree and call them simply corrections or retracements.

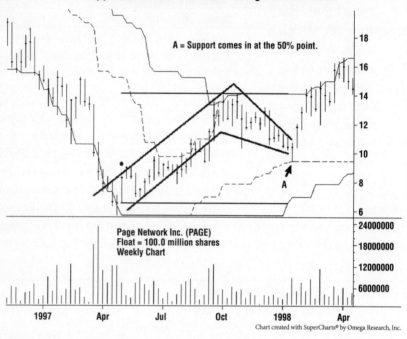

Figure 2-27   **The Upright Flag Formation with Support at 50% of the Float—Page Network Inc.**

A = Support comes in at the 50% point.

A

Page Network Inc. (PAGE)
Float = 100.0 million shares
Weekly Chart

Chart created with SuperCharts® by Omega Research, Inc.

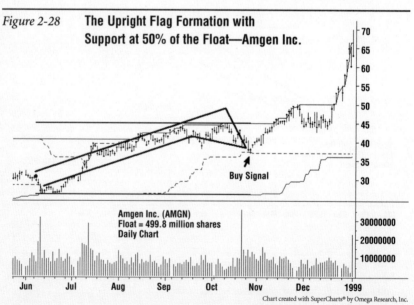

Figure 2-28   **The Upright Flag Formation with Support at 50% of the Float—Amgen Inc.**

Buy Signal

Amgen Inc. (AMGN)
Float = 499.8 million shares
Daily Chart

Chart created with SuperCharts® by Omega Research, Inc.

float finding support from the bottom half. (See chapter 4 for a detailed discussion of this idea of support and resistance at the midway point in the float turnover.) Good examples of upright flag formations include Novell (NOVL), Page Network (PAGE), and Amgen (AMGN) (see figures 2-26, 2-27, and 2-28). The bold diagonal lines on these charts highlight the flag formations.

Discovery 9

Price resistance in down-trends occurs as a stock's price rises to the 50% point in the float turnover price range giving rise to inverted flag formations with a sell point.

The Inverted Flag Formation

The inverted or upside-down flag is the exact opposite of the upright flag and is found near tops and in down-trends. These formations create trading opportunities to short a stock. *Shorting* is a transaction in which one sells borrowed stock and buys it back at a lower price to make a profit. It follows the principle of trying to buy low and sell high, but one simply sells first and buys later.

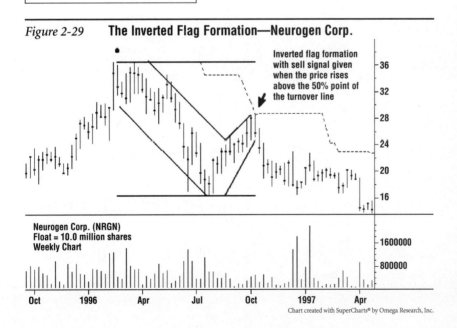

Figure 2-29   **The Inverted Flag Formation—Neurogen Corp.**

Chart created with SuperCharts® by Omega Research, Inc.

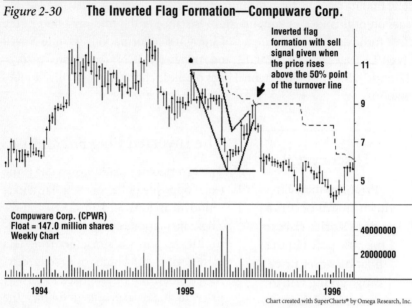

Figure 2-30   The Inverted Flag Formation—Compuware Corp.

Inverted flag formation with sell signal given when the price rises above the 50% point of the turnover line

Compuware Corp. (CPWR)
Float = 147.0 million shares
Weekly Chart

Chart created with SuperCharts® by Omega Research, Inc.

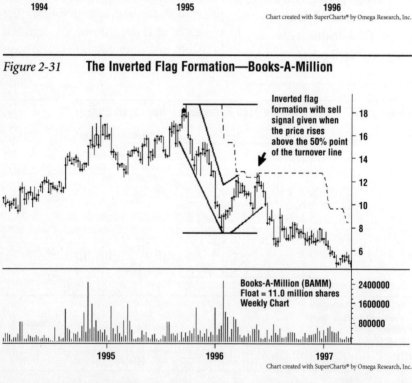

Figure 2-31   The Inverted Flag Formation—Books-A-Million

Inverted flag formation with sell signal given when the price rises above the 50% point of the turnover line

Books-A-Million (BAMM)
Float = 11.0 million shares
Weekly Chart

Chart created with SuperCharts® by Omega Research, Inc.

The opportunity to short arises when the stock's price stalls and reverses direction at the 50% point in the float's turnover. This stalling action occurs because of overhead supply. Three excellent examples of inverted flags are Neurogen Corp. (NRGN), Compuware Corp. (CPWR), and Books-A-Million (BAMM) (see figures 2-29, 2-30, and 2-31).

Discovery 10

Price resistance in down-trends following a topping formation occurs as a stock's price rises above the float turnover price range, thus giving rise to weak bases of support with a breakout to the upside sell point.

The Weak Base of Support Formation

The *weak base of support* formation most commonly occurs in down-trends after a stock has formed a top and its price heads lower. The weak base usually (but not always) forms considerably lower than the final turnover at the top. For a short period in the long *downward move*, the price goes sideways and looks like it is forming a new base of support at

Figure 2-32   **The Weak Base of Support Formation—
RealNetworks Inc.**

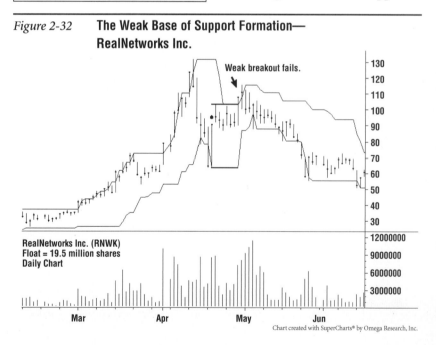

Chart created with SuperCharts® by Omega Research, Inc.

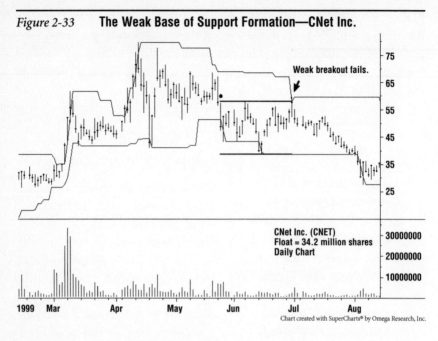

Figure 2-33 **The Weak Base of Support Formation—CNet Inc.**

Weak breakout fails.

CNet Inc. (CNET)
Float = 34.2 million shares
Daily Chart

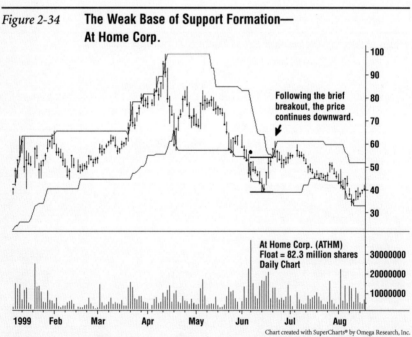

Figure 2-34 **The Weak Base of Support Formation—At Home Corp.**

Following the brief breakout, the price continues downward.

At Home Corp. (ATHM)
Float = 82.3 million shares
Daily Chart

a bottom or in a correction. After the sideways base of support is complete, the price attempts to move back to the upside. It rises briefly above the float turnover only to fail miserably.

The buyers in the sideways move are apparently not holding their shares tightly because the stock's price moves lower. In other words, the break-out fails because the support under the price is too weak to support an upward move. Thus, the price reverses direction and heads lower once again. If we carefully watch the price action at this breakout point, an opportunity arises for shorting the stock. Examples are RealNetworks (RNWK), CNet (CNET), and At Home Corp. (ATHM) (see figures 2-32, 2-33, and 2-34).

CHAPTER THREE

Technicals 101:
How to Understand — and Profit from — the Indicators

... for the sun didn't revolve around the earth but instead the earth revolved around the sun.

N ow that I've introduced float analysis, its discoveries, and a variety of float turnover formations, this chapter focus on the technical basis of float turnovers. These include the common characteristics of float turnovers, the relationship of a stock's present price to its float turnover, and trending characteristics. To prepare for this discussion, I will briefly cover the three indicators used in float analysis. Two of them were introduced in chapter 1 and will be briefly discussed again.

The Cumulative-Volume Float Indicators

As I mentioned in chapter 1, there are three indicators used in float analysis. Jan is a trading software developer and certified Omega Research solution provider. Presently, there are three stock indicators used in analyzing float turnovers.[11] Each of these indicators serves a different purpose and gives us

---

11 The software for these indicators works exclusively as an add-on to Omega Research's SuperCharts and TradeStation charting software platform.

a different perspective on tracking the float as well as alerting us when specific float turnover formations have arisen. They are:

- *The Cumulative-Volume Float Indicator*
- *The Cumulative-Volume Percentage Indicator*
- *The Cumulative-Volume Channel Indicator*

The float and channel indicators are created by cumulatively adding volume numbers in a backward-in-time direction. The percentage indicator is created by cumulatively adding volume numbers in a forward-in-time direction.

The Cumulative-Volume Float Indicator

A cumulative-volume float indicator tracks the float turnover by adding volume numbers cumulatively in a reverse chronological direction starting from any given date.

After locating the float number for a particular stock that I want to track, I manually enter this number into the indicator's software.[12] The computer then plots the float lines and the dot properly. The lines and dot are determined by adding cumulatively all volume numbers beginning with a given day's end-of-day volume with the previous day's volume and adding the total of these to the next volume number going backward in time. The indicator's software keeps adding the volume numbers cumulatively until it reaches the day on which the cumulative total is equal to the float number that was entered.

12 The float numbers have to be entered manually because a reliable data feed that provides end-of-day data (open, high, low, and closing prices with volume of trades) as well as the stock's current float number cannot be found at present. For NASDAQ stocks, I double the size of the inputted float number because, as was noted in chapter 1, the NASDAQ doubles its volume calculations. (For sources of stock float numbers, see footnote 3 on page 2.) If the float number for a company I'm tracking changes because of a stock split, for example, the inputted float number must be changed as well.

Figure 3-1   **The Cumulative-Volume Float Indicator**

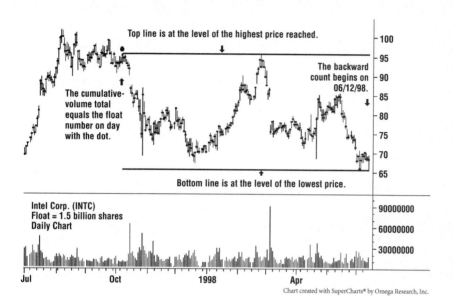

When the software finds the date where one complete float turnover has occurred, it places a dot above that bar on the chart. The dot denotes the time range on the float turnover. Then it plots the price range of the float turnover by placing two horizontal lines like those on the Xicor charts in chapter 1. These lines are placed at the levels that correspond with the highest and lowest prices during this backward count. The lines also act as triggers (if the indicator is set to a current date setting) to give alerts when the price moves up through the top line or moves down through the bottom line. As an example, the chart of Intel Corp. (INTC) shows how the cumulative-volume float indicator looked at close of day on June 12, 1998 (see figure 3-1). The cumulative-volume count continues backward in time to October 8, 1997.

The cumulative-volume float indicator tracks the float by putting a dot above the historical price bar, which represents the point from which the total float has turned over. It also places two horizontal lines corresponding to the highest and lowest prices reached during this reverse chronological count, and it gives alerts when the price breaks through either line. It is most effective for finding stocks making bottoms or tops, as it alerts you to stocks that are breaking out after forming a bottom turnover base as well as stocks that have formed a turnover top and are breaking below the float turnover.

The Cumulative-Volume Percentage Indicator

The second indicator used to track float turnovers is the cumulative-volume percentage indicator. Here, we'll study the float turnover in a histogram format. When Jan and I were collaborating on this indicator, I told him I wanted an indicator that would start tracking the float from the current day's date and would alert me on the day in the future in which the cumulative trading volume equaled the floating supply of shares. I wanted to be able to know when a stock that was making a fast move to the upside was nearing the completion of its float turnover, as this often corresponds to the precise top of the move. Remember the dramatic move that Xicor made after its price had turned upward and its cumulative trading volume equaled its float (see chapter 1, figure 1-20).

> A cumulative-volume percentage indicator tracks the float turnover by adding volume numbers cumulatively in a forward chronological direction starting from any given date. It is plotted as a histogram on a percentage of the float basis.

If I had entered the beginning date into this second percentage indicator, I would have received an alert when the float turnover hit 100%, corresponding with the top of the price move (see figure 3-2).

To get a clear sense of the percentage indicator, look at a couple of examples, again focusing on Xicor. Figures 3-3 and 3-4 show how the indicator would have looked at different times in the price move.

Because stocks that are making very fast moves to the upside often go through one complete float turnover, this indicator is an excellent tool to alert us when the move is completed.

Figure 3-2   The Cumulative-Volume Percentage Indicator— 100% Float Turnover

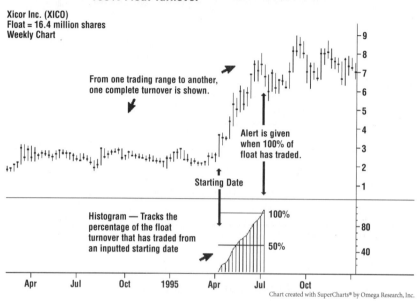

Xicor Inc. (XICO)
Float = 16.4 million shares
Weekly Chart

From one trading range to another, one complete turnover is shown.

Alert is given when 100% of float has traded.

Starting Date

Histogram — Tracks the percentage of the float turnover that has traded from an inputted starting date

100%

50%

Apr   Jul   Oct   1995   Apr   Jul   Oct

Chart created with SuperCharts® by Omega Research, Inc.

Figure 3-3   The Cumulative-Volume Percentage Indicator— 40% Float Turnover

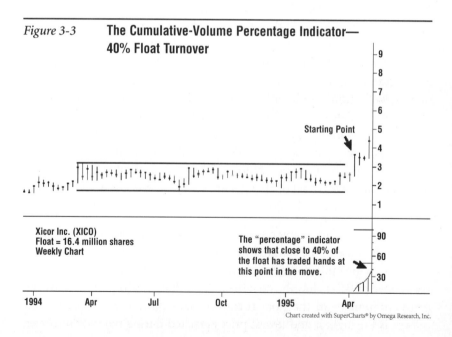

Starting Point

Xicor Inc. (XICO)
Float = 16.4 million shares
Weekly Chart

The "percentage" indicator shows that close to 40% of the float has traded hands at this point in the move.

1994   Apr   Jul   Oct   1995   Apr

Chart created with SuperCharts® by Omega Research, Inc.

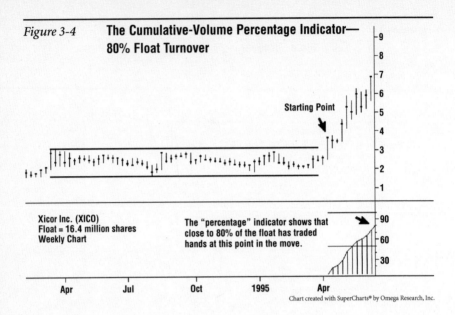

Figure 3-4   **The Cumulative-Volume Percentage Indicator—80% Float Turnover**

Starting Point

Xicor Inc. (XICO)
Float = 16.4 million shares
Weekly Chart

The "percentage" indicator shows that close to 80% of the float has traded hands at this point in the move.

Apr   Jul   Oct   1995   Apr

Chart created with SuperCharts® by Omega Research, Inc.

The Cumulative-Volume Channel Indicator

The third indicator came into existence because I was having a frustrating experience trying to study float turnovers historically. I wanted to be able to study float turnovers just before big moves to the upside, and I wanted an easy way of finding them. When I looked at a chart and saw that prices had bottomed and turned around, I wondered just where the float would fit into that bottom, but in order to find it, I had to replot my two lines and dot at various dates to find the proper place where it would fit. I found this both time-consuming and frustrating, so I talked to Jan about the problem and he came up with a solution. What he did was ingenious. By thinking of those top and bottom lines of the original float indicator on a **continuum basis**, he created a set of channel lines that showed just where the price breaks above or below the float.

As was discussed in chapter 1, it's called the *cumulative-volume channel indicator* because of the channel-like image formed by the lines plotted on the graph. This indicator is extremely useful to show when a stock's price rises above or falls below the float turnover. It does this by plotting **only the price component of the float turnover**. Remember that the price component is the highest and lowest prices reached during the float turnover.

Figure 3-5   **The Cumulative-Volume Channel Indicator**

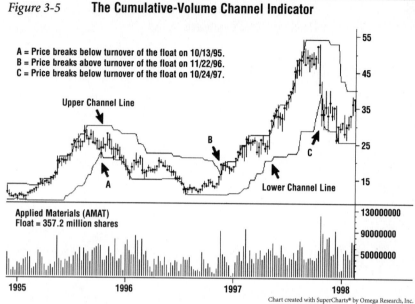

A = Price breaks below turnover of the float on 10/13/95.
B = Price breaks above turnover of the float on 11/22/96.
C = Price breaks below turnover of the float on 10/24/97.

Applied Materials (AMAT)
Float = 357.2 million shares

Chart created with SuperCharts® by Omega Research, Inc.

Thus, the channel lines are created by plotting two points on the same vertical axis as the price bar. One point is plotted at the present float turnover's

> The cumulative-volume channel indicator is extremely useful to show when a stock's price rises above or falls below the float turnover by plotting only the price component of the float turnover.

highest prices, and one point is plotted at the lowest price. These points are calculated on a bar-to-bar basis, which when connected together, form the continuum channel lines. A good example of channel lines is the chart of Applied Materials (AMAT) (see figure 3-5).

This chart shows two channel lines. Notice that sometimes the price is above both lines, sometimes it's below both lines, and sometimes it's between the two channel lines. On the far left of the chart we see that the price is rising; it tops in the middle of August 1995, then turns down and crosses below the bottom channel line in the week of October 13, 1995. The price then gradually declines for almost a year and bottoms in late July 1996. It then forms a bottom pattern and breaks above the float turnover on November 22, 1996.

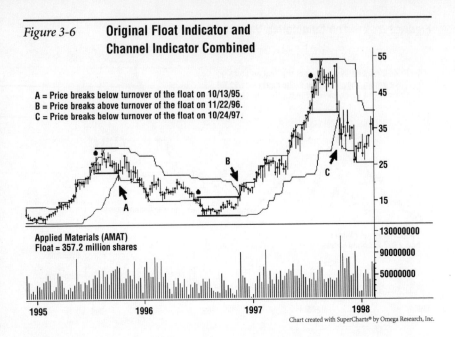

Figure 3-6   **Original Float Indicator and**
                 Channel Indicator Combined

A = Price breaks below turnover of the float on 10/13/95.
B = Price breaks above turnover of the float on 11/22/96.
C = Price breaks below turnover of the float on 10/24/97.

Applied Materials (AMAT)
Float = 357.2 million shares

Chart created with SuperCharts® by Omega Research, Inc.

The price continues to rise, topping in late August 1997. When the top formation is complete, the price breaks through the bottom channel line on October 24, 1997. These three dates (October 13, 1995, November 22, 1996, and October 24, 1997) are the points on this chart where the price breaks above and below the float turnover.

> The channel indicator simply plots one point at the present float turnover's highest price and one point at the lowest price. These points are calculated on a bar-to-bar basis, which when connected together form the continuum channel lines.

To better understand how this channel indicator is created, remember that every day that the float is calculated there are two price levels corresponding to the highest and lowest prices in the float turnover price range. This indicator simply plots those high and low prices each day and connects them from one day to the next so they form continuous lines. Looking at any price bar, we can see where the highest and lowest points in the float turnover were at that bar (see figure 3-6).

The Channel Lines at a 50% Setting

The channel indicator can be set to track all of the float or some percentage of it. Tracking half, or 50%, of the float has become standard practice in float analysis, as I have discovered that there is a natural tendency of stocks to find support or resistance when the price moves to these levels. Throughout this book, all charts with solid channel lines are set to 100% of the float, while broken channel lines represent 50% of the float. For an example, look at figure 3-7, a chart of Applied Materials (AMAT). The discovery that there is a natural support or resistance point at 50% of the float will be discussed thoroughly in chapter 4.

The Common Characteristics of Float Turnovers

Float analysis charts can be described and classified by numerous characteristics. I have chosen to discuss those characteristics that I feel are most commonly seen. These include time duration, float size, price to price-range relationships, and trending characteristics.

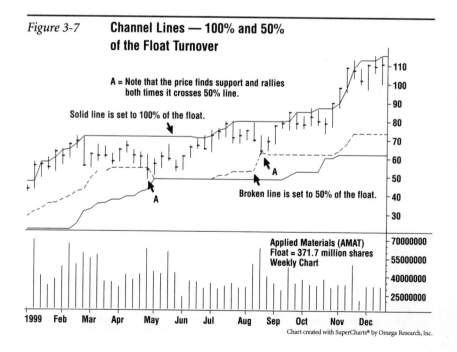

Figure 3-7   **Channel Lines — 100% and 50% of the Float Turnover**

A = Note that the price finds support and rallies both times it crosses 50% line.

Solid line is set to 100% of the float.

Broken line is set to 50% of the float.

Applied Materials (AMAT)
Float = 371.7 million shares
Weekly Chart

Chart created with SuperCharts® by Omega Research, Inc.

Time Duration and Float Size

The time length and float size for float turnovers are clearly quite diverse. No two stocks are exactly the same. They range from stocks with small floats that take a long time for a float turnover to occur to stocks with big floats that have rapidly occurring float turnovers. Looking at different examples often surprises newcomers to float analysis. Few people realize just how fast float turnovers can occur, even for well-known stocks.

> The time length and float size for float turnovers are quite diverse. They can range from stocks with small floats with both slow and fast turnovers to big floats with both long and rapid turnovers.

Small Float / Slow Turnover

This type of float turnover is found on thinly traded stocks of small companies. As the title implies, these companies have very few shares available for trading, and the rate of trading the entire float is quite slow. Optical Coating Labs (OCLI) is an example, with 9.0 million shares; its float turnover goes back 22 months (see figure 3-8).

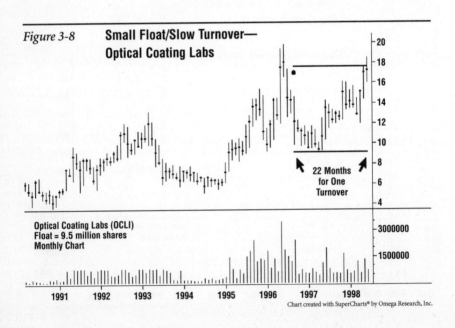

Figure 3-8   **Small Float/Slow Turnover— Optical Coating Labs**

Optical Coating Labs (OCLI)
Float = 9.5 million shares
Monthly Chart

22 Months for One Turnover

Chart created with SuperCharts® by Omega Research, Inc.

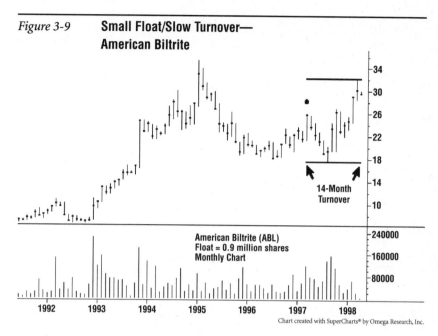

Figure 3-9   **Small Float/Slow Turnover—
American Biltrite**

Another example is American Biltrite (ABL). It has just 900,000 shares to trade, and a recent turnover took 14 months (see figure 3-9).

Small Float / Fast Turnover

In spring 1998, several small Internet-related companies with small float numbers had big run-ups with extremely rapid turnovers. Some stocks were having float turnovers several times in one day. This was the first time I had ever seen this phenomenon. Day traders must have been extremely busy on these days of high speculation. The most extreme case was a company called K-tel (KTEL). With a small float of 1.7 million shares, this company had one day when 14 million shares were traded. So it had eight float turnovers in one trading day, or approximately one float turnover every 47 minutes (see figure 3-10).

> **Small floats with slow or fast turnovers are found on thinly traded stocks of small companies.**

Another example of a stock with a small float having rapid turnovers is ProNet Link (PNLK) (see figure 3-11). In just a matter of days, it had trading volume that equaled its float.

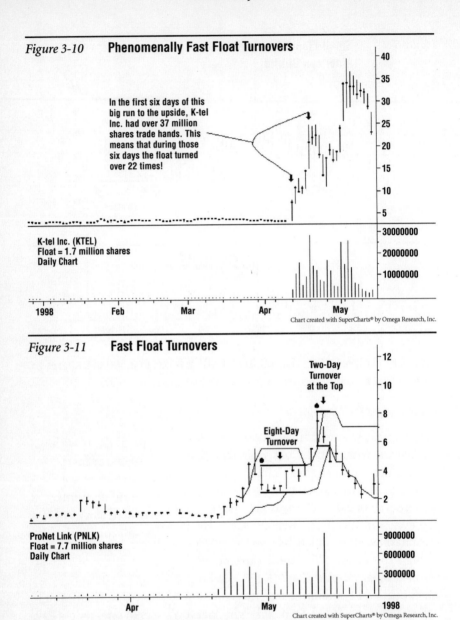

Figure 3-10   **Phenomenally Fast Float Turnovers**

In the first six days of this big run to the upside, K-tel Inc. had over 37 million shares trade hands. This means that during those six days the float turned over 22 times!

K-tel Inc. (KTEL)
Float = 1.7 million shares
Daily Chart

1998   Feb   Mar   Apr   May

Chart created with SuperCharts® by Omega Research, Inc.

Figure 3-11   **Fast Float Turnovers**

Two-Day Turnover at the Top

Eight-Day Turnover

ProNet Link (PNLK)
Float = 7.7 million shares
Daily Chart

Apr   May   1998

Chart created with SuperCharts® by Omega Research, Inc.

After the bear market of 1998, stocks of Internet companies roared to new highs. Ebay (EBAY) was one such company. One of the top stocks for 1998, its cumulative volume equaled its float every three to five days (see figure 3-12).

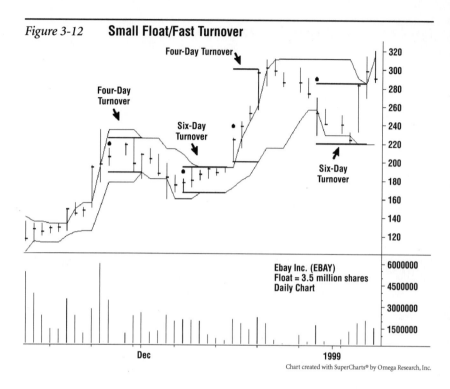

Figure 3-12   **Small Float/Fast Turnover**

Four-Day Turnover

Four-Day
Turnover

Six-Day
Turnover

Six-Day
Turnover

Ebay Inc. (EBAY)
Float = 3.5 million shares
Daily Chart

Dec   1999

Chart created with SuperCharts® by Omega Research, Inc.

Big Float / Slow Turnover

This type of float turnover occurs in the largest companies in the stock market. They have huge floats that take years to complete one turnover. Two good examples with floats that have shares running into the billions are General Electric (GE) and Coca Cola (KO) (see figures 3-13 and 3-14).

> **Big floats with long or rapid turnovers occur in the largest companies in the stock market.**

Big Float / Fast Turnover

In this category, we must qualify the term *fast turnover*. Whereas most companies with large floats will take a year or more to form a float turnover, here we find the float turnover occurring in a relatively short period of months. I have yet to find a really large float turning over in a matter of weeks. Two well-known companies with large floats that have been known to turn over rapidly are Cisco Systems (CSCO) and Intel Corp. (INTC) (see figures 3-15 and 3-16).

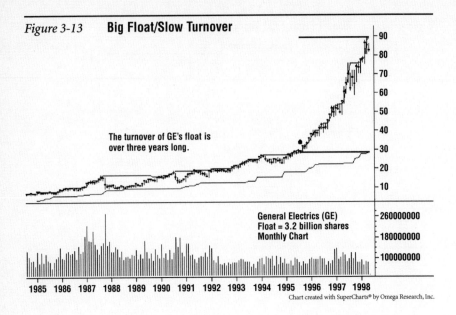

Figure 3-13   **Big Float/Slow Turnover**

The turnover of GE's float is
over three years long.

General Electrics (GE)
Float = 3.2 billion shares
Monthly Chart

Chart created with SuperCharts® by Omega Research, Inc.

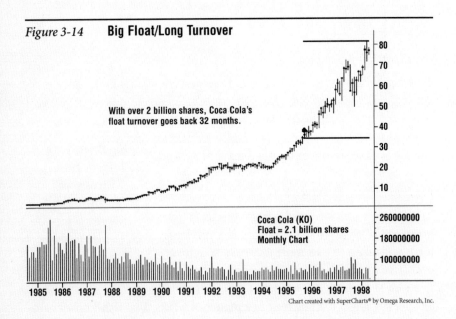

Figure 3-14   **Big Float/Long Turnover**

With over 2 billion shares, Coca Cola's
float turnover goes back 32 months.

Coca Cola (KO)
Float = 2.1 billion shares
Monthly Chart

Chart created with SuperCharts® by Omega Research, Inc.

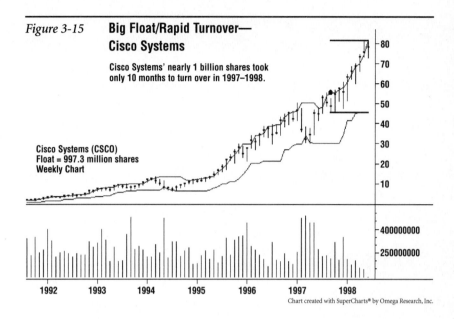

Figure 3-15 **Big Float/Rapid Turnover—Cisco Systems**

Cisco Systems' nearly 1 billion shares took only 10 months to turn over in 1997–1998.

Cisco Systems (CSCO)
Float = 997.3 million shares
Weekly Chart

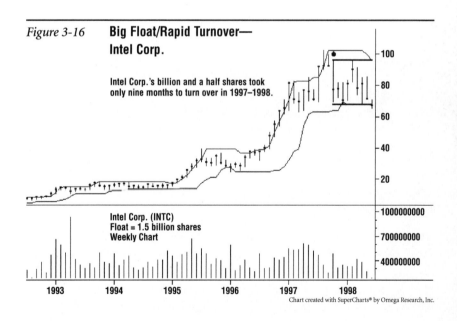

Figure 3-16 **Big Float/Rapid Turnover—Intel Corp.**

Intel Corp.'s billion and a half shares took only nine months to turn over in 1997–1998.

Intel Corp. (INTC)
Float = 1.5 billion shares
Weekly Chart

Price to Price-Range Relationship

The relationship between a stock's present price and its present float turnover price range is vital in float analysis. It is one thing to look at a stock's float turnover with the 20/20 vision of hindsight. It is quite another to analyze the stock properly in real time. When tracking float turnovers, it's the relationship between the present price to the float turnover price range that is crucial. Any price on the chart has a relationship to the float turnover price range of which it is part. It can be near the top, middle, or bottom. If the current price is near the bottom of its float turnover price range, there are a lot of people who are holding losing positions. They represent resistance to an upward move in prices because when the price gets up to the level at which they bought, they might want to sell just to break even. As discussed in chapter 1, this is called overhead resistance, or overhead supply. If a stock's price is near the top of the float turnover price range, the buyers underneath the price are holding *winning positions*. They represent a floor or base of support under the present price. The theory is that if the price comes down to the level at which they bought, they will want to buy some more. The float analysis indicators track the present price in relation to the float turnover's price range. This helps to determine how much overhead resistance is above it or how much support is below it.

> It is the relationship between the present price to the float turnover price range that is crucial when tracking float turnovers.

Trending Characteristics — The Staircase Model of Price Movements

I remember listening to an audio tape produced by *Investor's Business Daily* in which legendary stock picker David Ryan talked about stocks making price moves to the upside in a staircase fashion. The cumulative-volume channel indicator provides a fine example of this staircase effect and is quite useful in tracking this phenomenon. Look at another chart of Applied Materials (AMAT) (see figure 3-17). Here we plainly see the staircase effect.

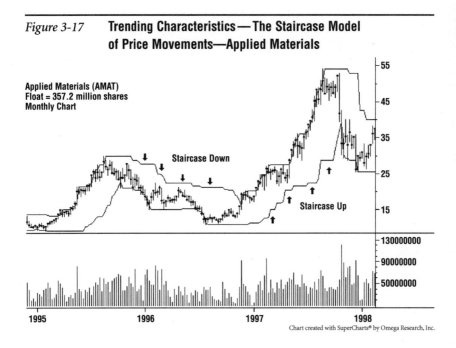

Figure 3-17   **Trending Characteristics — The Staircase Model of Price Movements—Applied Materials**

Another example is seen on a chart of Ascend Communications (ASND). It was in a long decline and then bottomed in late 1997. When it turned around, so did its float turnover staircase (see figure 3-18).

A second way to view this staircase effect during long upward or downward price moves is to plot the float indicator in a back-to-back stacking formation. Good examples of this are seen on the charts of Safeway (SWY) and Micron Technology (MU) (see figures 3-19 and 3-20).

> **The cumulative-volume channel indicator provides a fine example of this staircase effect and is quite useful in tracking this phenomenon.**

Recognizing that the float turns over many times during long upward price trends or long downward price trends presents a completely new way of thinking about support and resistance on price and volume charts. In the next chapter, we will see how float analysis actually expands the traditional definitions of support and resistance and creates a new model of stock behavior.

Figure 3-18

**Trending Characteristics — The Staircase Model
of Price Movements — Ascend Communications**

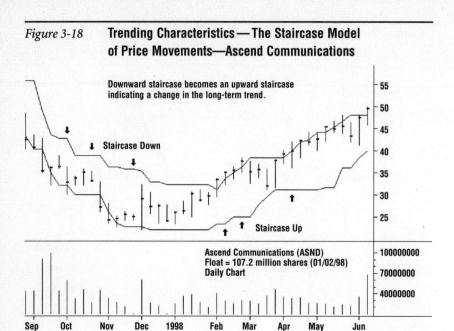

Downward staircase becomes an upward staircase
indicating a change in the long-term trend.

Staircase Down

Staircase Up

Ascend Communications (ASND)
Float = 107.2 million shares (01/02/98)
Daily Chart

Chart created with SuperCharts® by Omega Research, Inc.

Figure 3-19

**Multiple Turnovers of the Float
in a Rising Price Trend**

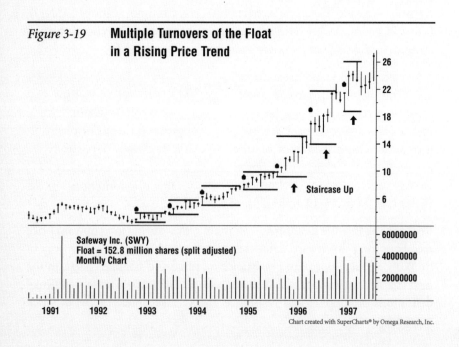

Staircase Up

Safeway Inc. (SWY)
Float = 152.8 million shares (split adjusted)
Monthly Chart

Chart created with SuperCharts® by Omega Research, Inc.

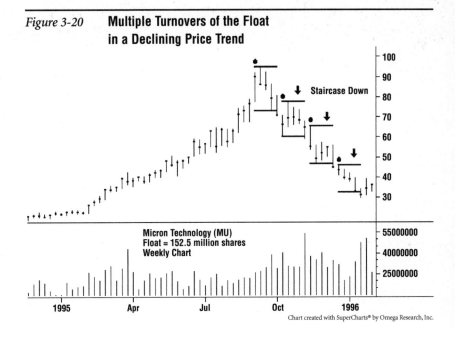

Figure 3-20 **Multiple Turnovers of the Float in a Declining Price Trend**

Staircase Down

Micron Technology (MU)
Float = 152.5 million shares
Weekly Chart

Chart created with SuperCharts® by Omega Research, Inc.

CHAPTER FOUR

Support and Resistance Redefined:

Creating a Model of Stock Behavior That Brings Results

. . . for with his new calculus, Newton could predict the movements of the moon.

The Rising Base of Support

The traditional view of a base of support in technical analysis is a sideways *price consolidation area* from which prices rise and which also offers support if the price drops back down to it. Xicor (XICO), the stock discussed in detail in chapter 1, gives an excellent example of this pattern.

Its price went sideways between $1 and $2 for two years and then rose above this area up to the $2 to $3 level. The initial $1 to $2 sideways consolidation area is considered a base of support from which the price rose. Once it has risen to a new level of $2 to $3, it finds support every time it comes back down close to the original basing area. Support also occurs when the price drops near a previous low during the $2 to $3 level (see figure 4-1).

In float analysis, a base of support includes this traditional view but also expands it in a new direction, so that a base of support is a constantly

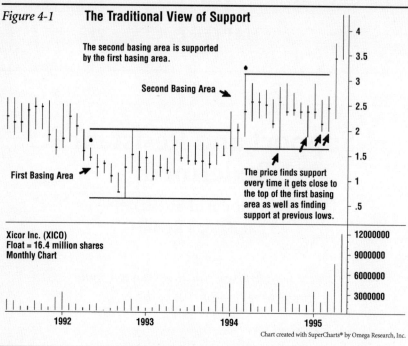

Figure 4-1 **The Traditional View of Support**

The second basing area is supported
by the first basing area.

Second Basing Area

First Basing Area

The price finds support
every time it gets close to
the top of the first basing
area as well as finding
support at previous lows.

Xicor Inc. (XICO)
Float = 16.4 million shares
Monthly Chart

12000000
9000000
6000000
3000000

1992   1993   1994   1995

Chart created with SuperCharts® by Omega Research, Inc.

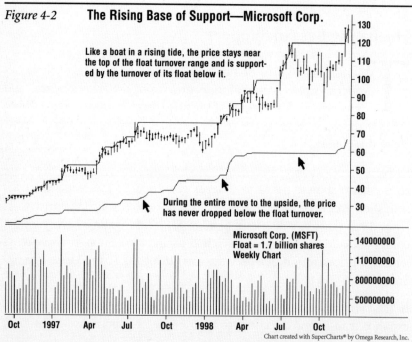

Figure 4-2 **The Rising Base of Support—Microsoft Corp.**

Like a boat in a rising tide, the price stays near
the top of the float turnover range and is supported by the turnover of its float below it.

During the entire move to the upside, the price
has never dropped below the float turnover.

Microsoft Corp. (MSFT)
Float = 1.7 billion shares
Weekly Chart

140000000
110000000
800000000
500000000

Oct   1997   Apr   Jul   Oct   1998   Apr   Jul   Oct

Chart created with SuperCharts® by Omega Research, Inc.

changing phenomenon that rises with a stock's price. Support then occurs when the float turnover is under the price: Stated another way, a stock's price is supported when it is rising above its float turnover.

A *strong base* of support starts as a sideways price consolidation area, but as the price rises, the base of support actually rises with it. More specifically, it rises underneath the price. Thus, when a stock's price is making a long upward move, the price will seemingly rise above the float. As new buyers bid the stock's price up, it becomes like a boat in a rising tide. Look at the chart of Microsoft Corp. (MSFT) (see figure 4-2): its price doesn't drop

> **A strong base of support starts as a sideways price consolidation area, but as the price rises, the base of support actually rises with it. More specifically, it rises underneath the price.**

below its float turnover at any point on the chart, but stays near the top of the float turnover price range during the entire upward move. Other good examples are Safeway (SWY) and EMC Corp. (EMC) (see figures 4-3 and 4-4).

Figure 4-3   **The Rising Base of Support—Safeway Inc.**

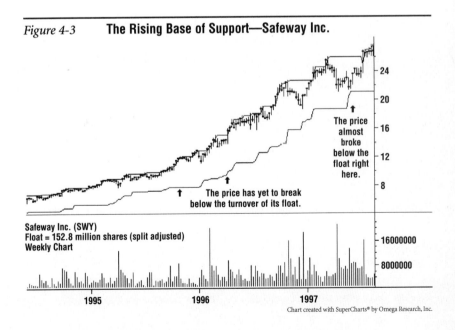

The price almost broke below the float right here.

The price has yet to break below the turnover of its float.

Safeway Inc. (SWY)
Float = 152.8 million shares (split adjusted)
Weekly Chart

1995   1996   1997

Chart created with SuperCharts® by Omega Research, Inc.

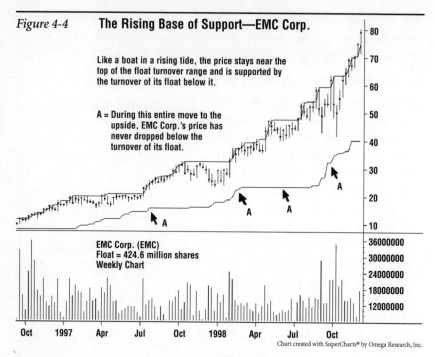

Figure 4-4   **The Rising Base of Support—EMC Corp.**

Like a boat in a rising tide, the price stays near the top of the float turnover range and is supported by the turnover of its float below it.

A = During this entire move to the upside, EMC Corp.'s price has never dropped below the turnover of its float.

EMC Corp. (EMC)
Float = 424.6 million shares
Weekly Chart

Chart created with SuperCharts® by Omega Research, Inc.

The Descending Ceiling of Resistance

In like manner, the traditional view of an area of resistance is defined as a sideways price consolidation area above a stock's present price. This congestion area causes resistance to any upward move and acts as a ceiling through which prices must struggle. In float analysis, it's this and more. Here, resistance is having the float turnover above the price.

> The ceiling of resistance follows descending prices and acts against rising prices throughout a long declining move.

This ceiling of resistance follows descending prices and acts against rising prices throughout a long declining move. The stock's price is like a boat going downstream with pressure coming from the float turnover that is above it. Novell (NOVL) (see figure 4-5) is in a long price decline with its float turnover providing pressure from above. Micron Technology (MU) is an excellent example of a stock having support on the way up and being under pressure on the way down (see figure 4-6).

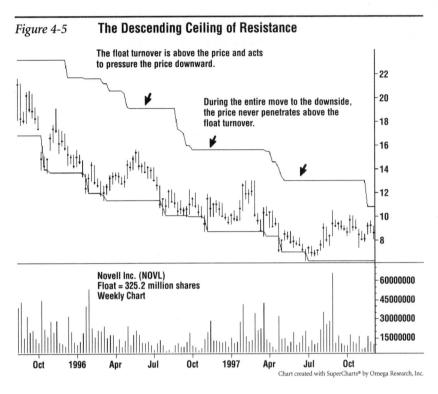

Figure 4-5 **The Descending Ceiling of Resistance**

The float turnover is above the price and acts to pressure the price downward.

During the entire move to the downside, the price never penetrates above the float turnover.

Novell Inc. (NOVL)
Float = 325.2 million shares
Weekly Chart

Chart created with SuperCharts® by Omega Research, Inc.

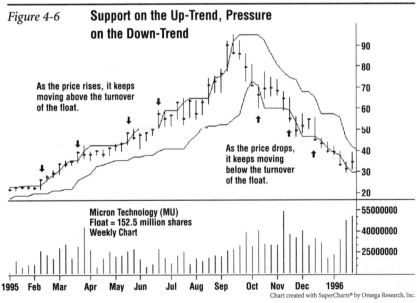

Figure 4-6 **Support on the Up-Trend, Pressure on the Down-Trend**

As the price rises, it keeps moving above the turnover of the float.

As the price drops, it keeps moving below the turnover of the float.

Micron Technology (MU)
Float = 152.5 million shares
Weekly Chart

Chart created with SuperCharts® by Omega Research, Inc.

Figure 4-7

The Base of Support Changes to the Ceiling of Resistance

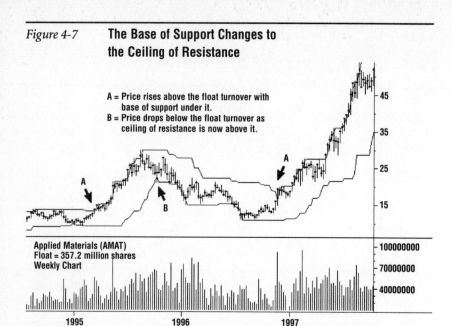

A = Price rises above the float turnover with base of support under it.
B = Price drops below the float turnover as ceiling of resistance is now above it.

Applied Materials (AMAT)
Float = 357.2 million shares
Weekly Chart

Chart created with SuperCharts® by Omega Research, Inc.

Figure 4-8

The Base of Support Changes to the Ceiling of Resistance and Back Again

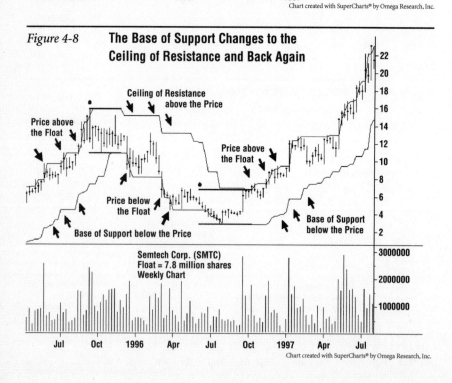

Ceiling of Resistance above the Price

Price above the Float

Price above the Float

Price below the Float

Base of Support below the Price

Base of Support below the Price

Semtech Corp. (SMTC)
Float = 7.8 million shares
Weekly Chart

Chart created with SuperCharts® by Omega Research, Inc.

The Changing Nature of Float Turnovers from Support to Resistance, and Vice Versa

Float turnovers are dynamic and constantly changing. They can move from being a base of support to a ceiling of resistance, and vice versa. Thus, whenever a stock in a long-term price decline turns around and starts heading back up, its float turnover will change from a ceiling of resistance to a base of support.

And likewise, when a stock in a long price up-trend turns around and starts heading down, its float turnover will change from a base of support to a ceiling of resistance. Applied Materials (AMAT) shows this well, as does Semtech Corp. (SMTC) (see figures 4-7 and 4-8).

> Whenever a stock in a long-term price decline turns around and starts heading back up, its float turnover will change from a ceiling of resistance to a base of support, and vice versa.

Unique Points of Support and Resistance in Up-Trends and Down-Trends

Price Reversals at the 50% Support Point — Support down under and Overhead Supply

There is a strong tendency for stock prices to find support or resistance halfway through the float turnover price range. This midway point in the float turnover is an area of great power. During long upward or downward moves, a stock's price will inevitably go against this long-term direction for short periods of time. Stocks going up have short downward price corrections, and stocks going down have short upward price *retracements*. A natural point of *price reversal* in this activity is the 50% level of the float turnover price range.

One way to see this is by plotting the historical channel indicator twice. One indicator is set at the actual float number, and the second is set to half this first number. When we do this, we find an amazing number of stocks correcting and retracing to this midway point in the float turnover. This

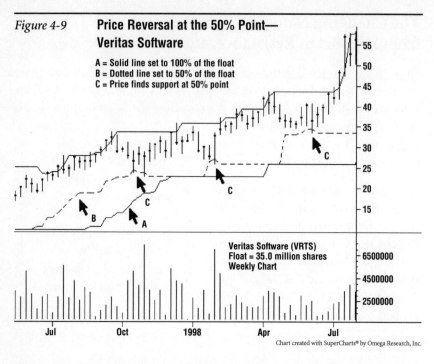

Figure 4-9 **Price Reversal at the 50% Point—Veritas Software**

A = Solid line set to 100% of the float
B = Dotted line set to 50% of the float
C = Price finds support at 50% point

B

A

C

C

C

Veritas Software (VRTS)
Float = 35.0 million shares
Weekly Chart

55
50
45
40
35
30
25
20
15

6500000
4500000
2500000

Jul   Oct   1998   Apr   Jul

Chart created with SuperCharts® by Omega Research, Inc.

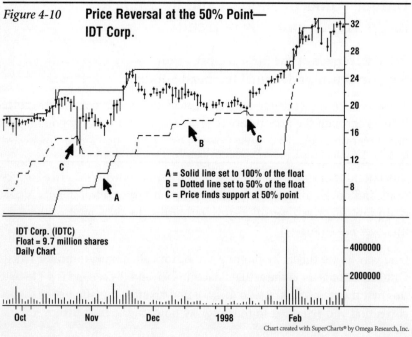

Figure 4-10 **Price Reversal at the 50% Point—IDT Corp.**

B

C

C

A

A = Solid line set to 100% of the float
B = Dotted line set to 50% of the float
C = Price finds support at 50% point

32
28
24
20
16
12
8

IDT Corp. (IDTC)
Float = 9.7 million shares
Daily Chart

4000000
2000000

Oct   Nov   Dec   1998   Feb

Chart created with SuperCharts® by Omega Research, Inc.

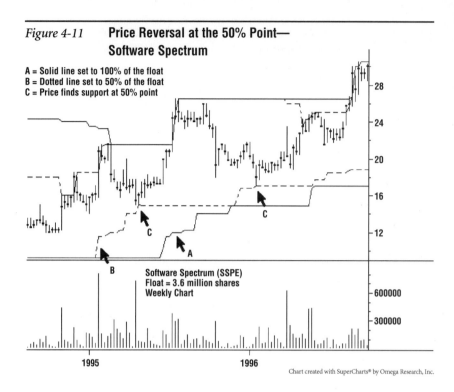

Figure 4-11   **Price Reversal at the 50% Point—
Software Spectrum**

A = Solid line set to 100% of the float
B = Dotted line set to 50% of the float
C = Price finds support at 50% point

Software Spectrum (SSPE)
Float = 3.6 million shares
Weekly Chart

Chart created with SuperCharts® by Omega Research, Inc.

midway point acts like a fulcrum for the forces of supply and demand. Good examples include Veritas Software (VRTS), IDT Corp. (IDTC), and Software Spectrum (SSPE) (see figures 4-9, 4-10, and 4-11).

Stocks that are making long downward price slides also have price reversals right at this mid-float point. Short rallies stall here as they run into overhead supply. In addition, stocks

> An amazing number of stocks correct and retrace at the 50% level of the float turnover price range. This midway point acts like a fulcrum for the forces of supply and demand.

that have topped and are heading lower often go through brief rallies to the upside that continue to the halfway point in the float turnover's price range and then resume their downward fall. Good examples of this include Applied Materials (AMAT), Inso Corp. (INSO), and Health Management Systems (HMSY) (see figures 4-12, 4-13, and 4-14).

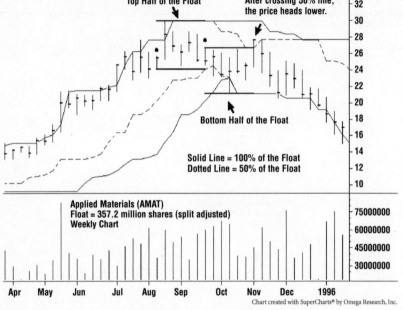

Figure 4-12   **Overhead Supply Occurring at 50% of the Float—Applied Materials**

Top Half of the Float

After crossing 50% line, the price heads lower.

Bottom Half of the Float

Solid Line = 100% of the Float
Dotted Line = 50% of the Float

Applied Materials (AMAT)
Float = 357.2 million shares (split adjusted)
Weekly Chart

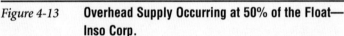

Chart created with SuperCharts® by Omega Research, Inc.

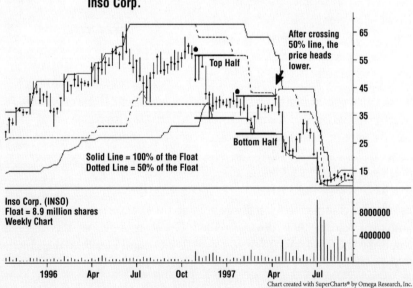

Figure 4-13   **Overhead Supply Occurring at 50% of the Float—Inso Corp.**

After crossing 50% line, the price heads lower.

Top Half

Bottom Half

Solid Line = 100% of the Float
Dotted Line = 50% of the Float

Inso Corp. (INSO)
Float = 8.9 million shares
Weekly Chart

Chart created with SuperCharts® by Omega Research, Inc.

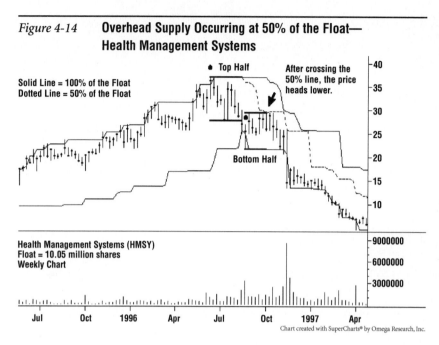

Figure 4-14 **Overhead Supply Occurring at 50% of the Float—Health Management Systems**

Thus, stocks in up-trends often correct downward, finding support at 50% of the float turnover, and stocks in down-trends often swing upward only to find resistance at this same 50% point. Support and resistance at the 50% level of the float turnover is one of the most potentially profitable phenomena in float analysis. Stock prices turning at these points are so common as to be seen on just about any stock you care to study.

> Support and resistance at the 50% level of the float turnover is one of the most potentially profitable phenomena in float analysis.

Price Reversals at the 100% Support Point — Overhead Support and Weak Bases

Although I just defined *support* as having a stock's float turnover underneath its price and *resistance* as having the float turnover above the price, there is one scenario in which (for a very brief period of time) this is not true. Here we find the stock's price acting in a rather peculiar fashion that

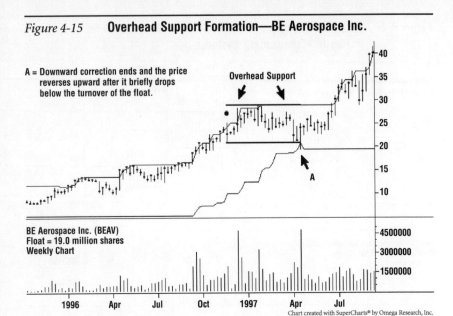

Figure 4-15 **Overhead Support Formation—BE Aerospace Inc.**

A = Downward correction ends and the price reverses upward after it briefly drops below the turnover of the float.

Overhead Support

A

BE Aerospace Inc. (BEAV)
Float = 19.0 million shares
Weekly Chart

Chart created with SuperCharts® by Omega Research, Inc.

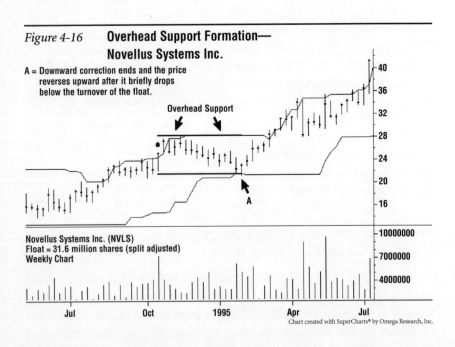

Figure 4-16 **Overhead Support Formation— Novellus Systems Inc.**

A = Downward correction ends and the price reverses upward after it briefly drops below the turnover of the float.

Overhead Support

A

Novellus Systems Inc. (NVLS)
Float = 31.6 million shares (split adjusted)
Weekly Chart

Chart created with SuperCharts® by Omega Research, Inc.

Figure 4-17   Overhead Support Formation—America Online

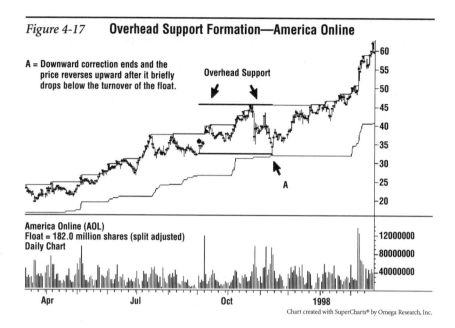

seems at first to defy logic. Viewing the float turnover as support when it's under a stock's price makes common sense, but is it possible for the float turnover to support the price when it is above it? Yes, there are short periods of time when a stock's price will briefly drop below the price range of its float turnover and suddenly begin to rise because the float turnover above the price is giving what I call *overhead support.* This can be understood in that the investors who bought above the stock's price are convinced that the stock is a long term value and they're holding their shares tightly.

> When the price drops below the float turnover, a price reversal occurs and the price moves up quite dramatically.

Thus, when the price drops below the float turnover, a price reversal occurs and the price moves up quite dramatically. Good examples of this are BE Aerospace (BEAV), Novellus Systems (NVLS), and America Online (AOL) (see figures 4-15, 4-16, and 4-17).

The reverse of this formation is seen in stocks that are trending downward and seemingly build a sideways base of support. But when the stock's price breaks above the base, it turns out to be a base of weakness as the price

> **When the stock's price breaks above the base, it turns out to be a base of weakness as the price immediately drops lower.**

immediately drops lower. The investors who bought at the lower prices within this float turnover are probably short-term traders who lack conviction and sell into the breakout to make a quick profit. Thus, the price goes lower. Wide bases of support often show this weakness. Without further buyers on the upside, the selling pressure brings the price down. Good examples of this are Advanced Micro Devices (AMD), Asyst (ASYT), and Battle Mountain Gold (BMG) (see figures 4-18, 4-19, and 4-20).

Support and Resistance in Multiple Turnover Sideways Bases

On occasion, after a stock makes a long price move in either an upward or downward direction, it will settle into a sideways formation for a long period of time. During these long basing formations, a most interesting and

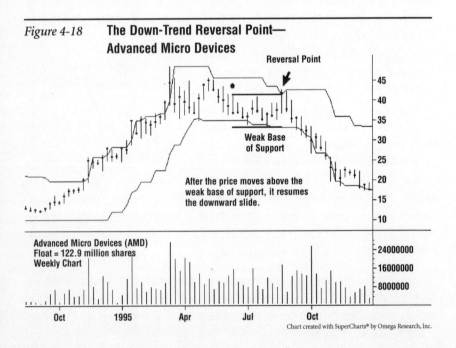

Figure 4-18 **The Down-Trend Reversal Point— Advanced Micro Devices**

Chart created with SuperCharts® by Omega Research, Inc.

Figure 4-19   **The Down-Trend Reversal Point—Asyst Inc.**

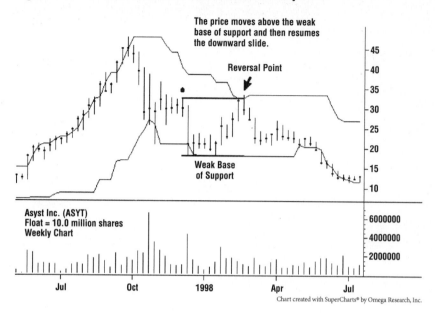

The price moves above the weak
base of support and then resumes
the downward slide.

Reversal Point

Weak Base
of Support

Asyst Inc. (ASYT)
Float = 10.0 million shares
Weekly Chart

Jul   Oct   1998   Apr   Jul

Chart created with SuperCharts® by Omega Research, Inc.

Figure 4-20   **The Down-Trend Reversal Point—
Battle Mountain Gold**

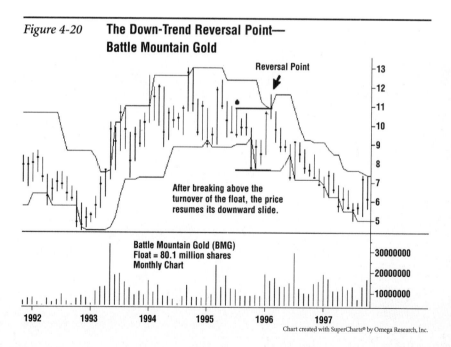

Reversal Point

After breaking above the
turnover of the float, the price
resumes its downward slide.

Battle Mountain Gold (BMG)
Float = 80.1 million shares
Monthly Chart

1992   1993   1994   1995   1996   1997

Chart created with SuperCharts® by Omega Research, Inc.

Figure 4-21   Double Turnover Sideways Base

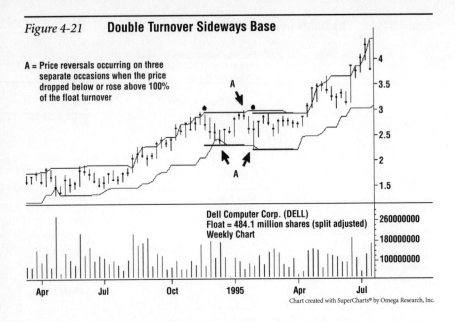

A = Price reversals occurring on three
separate occasions when the price
dropped below or rose above 100%
of the float turnover

A

A

Dell Computer Corp. (DELL)
Float = 484.1 million shares (split adjusted)
Weekly Chart

4
3.5
3
2.5
2
1.5

260000000
180000000
100000000

Apr   Jul   Oct   1995   Apr   Jul

Chart created with SuperCharts® by Omega Research, Inc.

Figure 4-22   Multiple Turnover Basing Formation

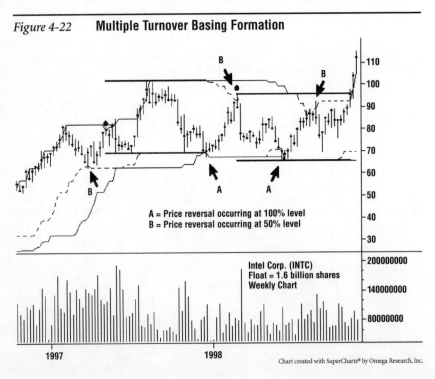

B

B

B

A = Price reversal occurring at 100% level
B = Price reversal occurring at 50% level

A   A

110
100
90
80
70
60
50
40
30

Intel Corp. (INTC)
Float = 1.6 billion shares
Weekly Chart

200000000
140000000
80000000

1997   1998

Chart created with SuperCharts® by Omega Research, Inc.

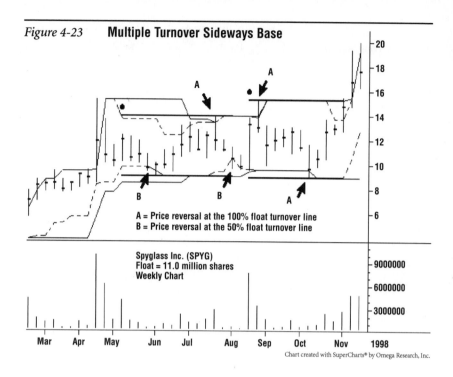

Figure 4-23   **Multiple Turnover Sideways Base**

A = Price reversal at the 100% float turnover line
B = Price reversal at the 50% float turnover line

Spyglass Inc. (SPYG)
Float = 11.0 million shares
Weekly Chart

Chart created with SuperCharts® by Omega Research, Inc.

potentially profitable situation occurs. Stuck in a trading range, the float will go through multiple float turnovers. During these multiple turnovers, the price will reverse direction right at the 50% and/or 100% levels. This occurs with amazing frequency. Good examples of this are Dell Computer Corp. (DELL), Intel Corp. (INTC), and Spyglass (SPYG) (see figures 4-21, 4-22, and 4-23).

> **During long basing formations, a float will go through multiple float turnovers and the price will reverse direction right at the 50% and/or 100% levels.**

Valid Breakouts

Whenever a stock's price emerges above a true base of support or drops below a true ceiling of resistance, we can always, in hindsight, find a valid breakout. Valid breakouts always precede long up-trends and long down-trends.

> **There are three distinct types of valid breakouts: breakouts that "don't look back," breakouts with corrections, and breakouts that occur after a multiple turnover sideways base.**

Valid breakouts demarcate the change from a ceiling of resistance to a base of support or vice versa, and they occur whenever the long-term *trend* changes direction. Thus, stocks with prices in long-term up-trends turn down and break out below the float turnover, and stocks with prices in long-term down-trends turn up and break out above the turnover. In each case, a new long-term trend gets under way with the valid breakout marking the beginning of the change. There are three distinct types of valid breakouts: breakouts that "don't look back," breakouts with corrections, and breakouts that occur after a multiple turnover sideways base.

The No-Looking-Back Breakout after a Long Down-Trend

Here we find the stock's price breaking above the float turnover and immediately heading higher, never again to enter the trading range from which it emerged. These stocks are usually, but not always, making fast runs to the upside. Three examples are Iomega Corp. (IOM), Recoton Corp. (RCOT), and Adelphia Com. (ADLAC) (see figures 4-24, 4-25, and 4-26).

Typically these breakouts occur on big volume, and they are not very common. More often, a stock's price is going to break above the top line and correct back down into the trading range preceding the breakout. Once the breakout occurs, the stock's price switches from having the float turnover above it acting as a ceiling of resistance to the float turnover becoming a base of support beneath it.

The No-Looking-Back Breakout after a Long Up-Trend

With stocks that have been in long up-trends, the no-looking-back breakout usually occurs in a short time frame and on heavy volume. Dropping below the float turnover, the stock's price doesn't return to the high levels

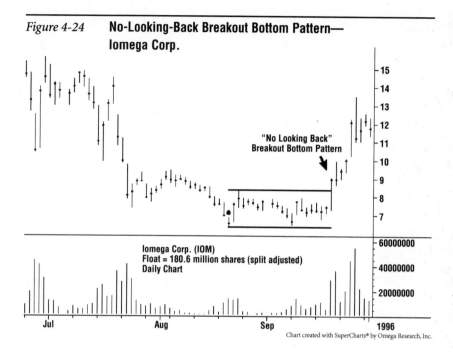

Figure 4-24   **No-Looking-Back Breakout Bottom Pattern— Iomega Corp.**

"No Looking Back" Breakout Bottom Pattern

Iomega Corp. (IOM)
Float = 180.6 million shares (split adjusted)
Daily Chart

Jul   Aug   Sep   **1996**

Chart created with SuperCharts® by Omega Research, Inc.

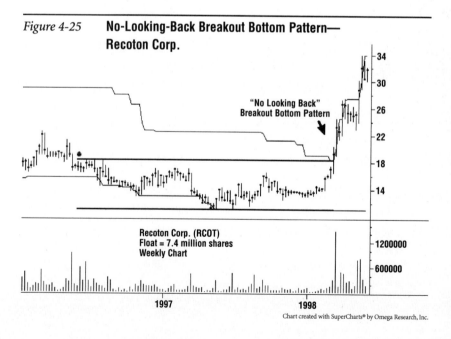

Figure 4-25   **No-Looking-Back Breakout Bottom Pattern— Recoton Corp.**

"No Looking Back" Breakout Bottom Pattern

Recoton Corp. (RCOT)
Float = 7.4 million shares
Weekly Chart

1997   **1998**

Chart created with SuperCharts® by Omega Research, Inc.

Figure 4-26 **No-Looking-Back Breakout Bottom Pattern—
Adelphia Com.**

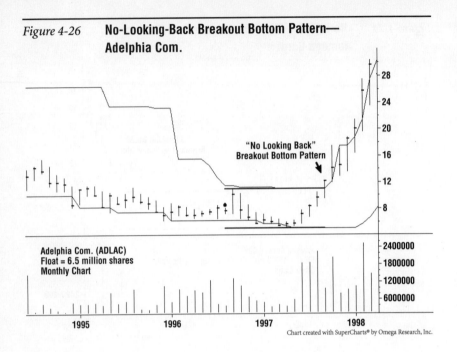

of days gone by. Novellus Sys. (NVLS), Chesapeake Energy (CHK), and Emulex Corp. (EMLX) are examples of this (see figures 4-27, 4-28, and 4-29). Once the breakout occurs, the float changes from a base of support under the stock's price to a ceiling of resistance.

It is quite common for a stock's price to cross above the float turnover only to come right back down into its previous trading range. Once the correction is completed, the price begins its climb upward.

Valid Breakouts with a Correction after a Long Down-Trend

It is quite common for a stock's price to cross above the float turnover only to come right back down into its previous trading range. Once the correction is completed, the price begins its climb upward. Electroglas (EGLS), Genesco (GCO), and Semtech Corp. (SMTC) are good examples of this pattern (see figures 4-30, 4-31, and 4-32).

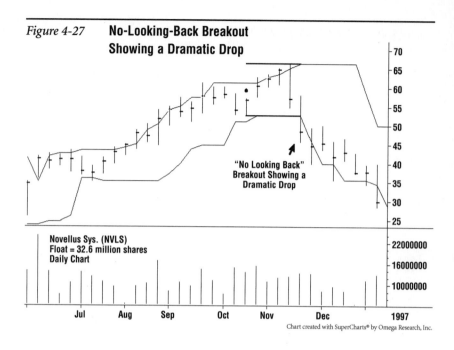

Figure 4-27   No-Looking-Back Breakout Showing a Dramatic Drop

"No Looking Back" Breakout Showing a Dramatic Drop

Novellus Sys. (NVLS)
Float = 32.6 million shares
Daily Chart

Chart created with SuperCharts® by Omega Research, Inc.

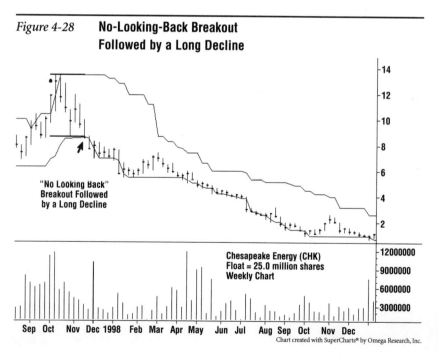

Figure 4-28   No-Looking-Back Breakout Followed by a Long Decline

"No Looking Back" Breakout Followed by a Long Decline

Chesapeake Energy (CHK)
Float = 25.0 million shares
Weekly Chart

Chart created with SuperCharts® by Omega Research, Inc.

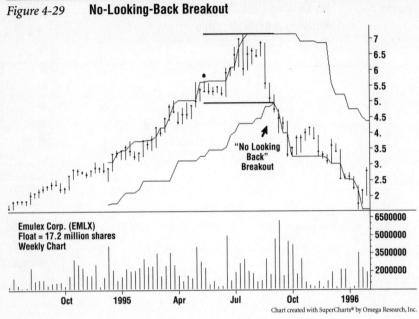

Figure 4-29   No-Looking-Back Breakout

Emulex Corp. (EMLX)
Float = 17.2 million shares
Weekly Chart

"No Looking Back" Breakout

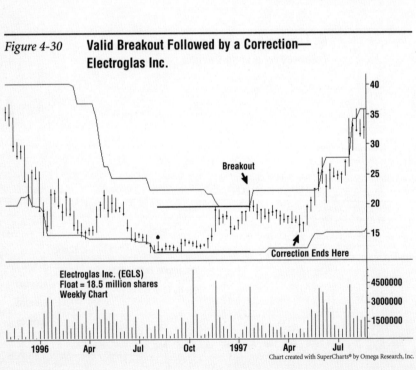

Figure 4-30   Valid Breakout Followed by a Correction—
Electroglas Inc.

Electroglas Inc. (EGLS)
Float = 18.5 million shares
Weekly Chart

Breakout

Correction Ends Here

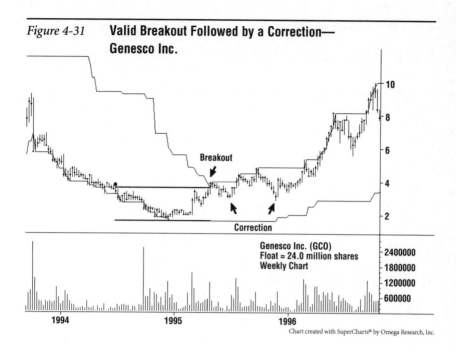

Figure 4-31   **Valid Breakout Followed by a Correction—
Genesco Inc.**

Breakout

Correction

Genesco Inc. (GCO)
Float = 24.0 million shares
Weekly Chart

2400000
1800000
1200000
600000

1994   1995   1996

Chart created with SuperCharts® by Omega Research, Inc.

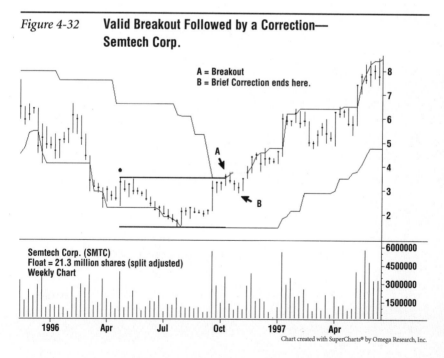

Figure 4-32   **Valid Breakout Followed by a Correction—
Semtech Corp.**

A = Breakout
B = Brief Correction ends here.

A

B

Semtech Corp. (SMTC)
Float = 21.3 million shares (split adjusted)
Weekly Chart

6000000
4500000
3000000
1500000

1996   Apr   Jul   Oct   1997   Apr

Chart created with SuperCharts® by Omega Research, Inc.

Valid Breakouts with a Retracement after a Long Up-Trend

In this pattern, like the previous one, the correction is upward, only to move downward soon thereafter. The stock's price breaks below the float turnover, then returns to its upward direction for a short retracement period only to turn south with plenty of momentum. Digital River (DRIV), Petsmart (PETM), and Advanced Micro Devices (AMD) are good examples of this type of breakout (see figures 4-33, 4-34, and 4-35).

Valid Breakouts after a Multiple Turnover Sideways Base

As previously noted, some stocks have sideways price moves in which the float turns over several times; these are the strongest of formations. At some point, the stock's price has a valid breakout either to the upside or the downside. Good examples include Lycos (LCOS), Spyglass (SPYG), and Iomega Corp. (IOM) (see figures 4-36, 4-37, and 4-38).

Figure 4-33 **Valid Breakout with a Retracement after a Long Up-Trend—Digital River Inc.**

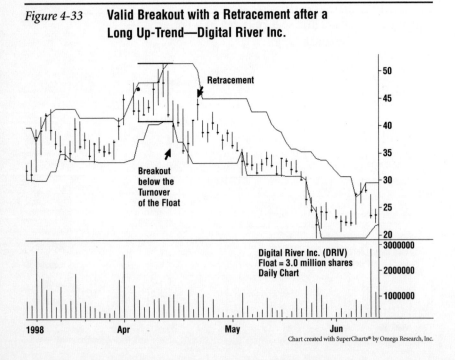

Chart created with SuperCharts® by Omega Research, Inc.

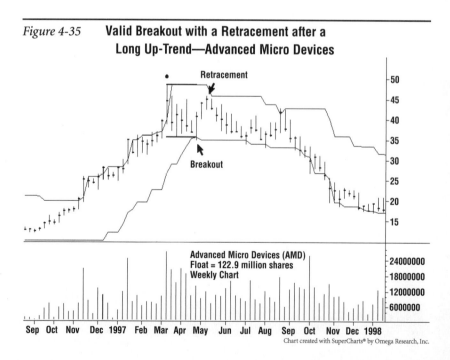

Figure 4-34 **Valid Breakout with a Retracement after a Long Up-Trend—Petsmart Inc.**

Retracement

Breakout below the Turnover of the Float

Petsmart Inc. (PETM)
Float = 72.8 million shares
Weekly Chart

1995   1996   1997

Chart created with SuperCharts® by Omega Research, Inc.

Figure 4-35 **Valid Breakout with a Retracement after a Long Up-Trend—Advanced Micro Devices**

Retracement

Breakout

Advanced Micro Devices (AMD)
Float = 122.9 million shares
Weekly Chart

Sep Oct Nov Dec 1997 Feb Mar Apr May Jun Jul Aug Sep Oct Nov Dec 1998

Chart created with SuperCharts® by Omega Research, Inc.

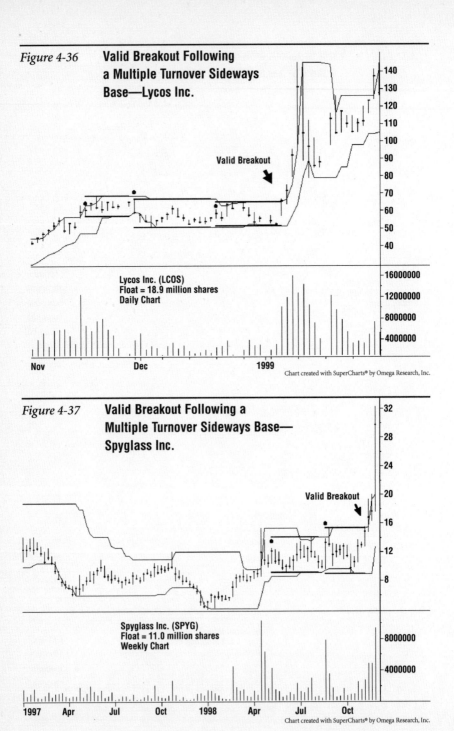

Figure 4-36

Valid Breakout Following a Multiple Turnover Sideways Base—Lycos Inc.

Valid Breakout

Lycos Inc. (LCOS)
Float = 18.9 million shares
Daily Chart

Chart created with SuperCharts® by Omega Research, Inc.

Figure 4-37

Valid Breakout Following a Multiple Turnover Sideways Base— Spyglass Inc.

Valid Breakout

Spyglass Inc. (SPYG)
Float = 11.0 million shares
Weekly Chart

Chart created with SuperCharts® by Omega Research, Inc.

Figure 4-38   **Valid Breakout Following a Multiple Turnover Sideways Base—Iomega Inc.**

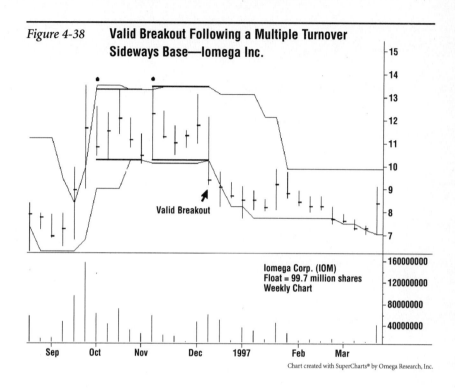

Iomega Corp. (IOM)
Float = 99.7 million shares
Weekly Chart

Valid Breakout

Chart created with SuperCharts® by Omega Research, Inc.

A Strategic Challenge

Valid breakouts and price reversal points are extremely powerful. But an obvious problem arises when attempting to use these signals in actual trading. I call it the *mirror image* problem. What looks like a valid breakout may turn out to be a reversal, and what looks like a reversal may turn out to be a valid breakout. When these signals occur, we never truly know which direction the stock is going to go. A sizable move may well be in the offing, but which direction it will take is not easy to determine. This, then, is float analysis's greatest challenge. Next, I'll discuss strategies to deal with the challenge as well as summarize float analysis as a model of price and volume behavior.

CHAPTER FIVE

Successful Strategies

That Made My Stock Portfolio Grow
Tenfold in Sixteen Months

*... and so it was a paradox, for light could be shown
to move as both a particle and a wave.*

The Mirror Image Dilemma and Its Solutions

Every stock indicator that was ever invented has its weaknesses. For example, it is well known that indicators that do well in trending markets won't do very well in sideways markets. And indicators that do well in sideways markets won't do very well in trending markets. The cumulative-volume float analysis indicators are also challenged by what I call the *mirror image* dilemma. The problem here is that everything in float analysis has a mirror image opposite. Thus, buy signals may or may not end up to have been buy signals, and sell signals may or may not end up to have been sell signals. What you think is a buy signal may turn out to have been a sell signal, and what you think is a sell signal may turn out to have been a buy signal.

For example, if we are tracking a stock that is making a long decline and it finally breaks out above its float turnover, we may be looking at a strong base of support or a weak base of support. It may be a no-looking-back breakout to the upside or a reversal with the price about to head much lower. Or if we are holding a high flier and its price drops below the turn-over of its float, it may be a no-looking-back breakout to the downside or it

121

may be an overhead support reversal point and about to head much higher. As you can see, everything we look at has the potential to be its opposite. Thus, as we might have expected, predicting price direction is not just a matter of buying when the price rises above a float turnover (although this is quite possible and often the case), or selling when it drops below the float turnover (although this is also quite possible and often the case).

Everything in float analysis has a mirror image opposite.

Do not think the problem is unsolvable and throw out float analysis altogether! I almost did that at one point, but fortunately I hung in there until I discovered the methods that worked for me. In the 16 months between September 1998 and January 2000, my portfolio made a tenfold increase. The only indicators I used were the float indicators talked about in this book. I can emphatically say that I solved the mirror image problem. The solution to this riddle has several key elements. Before discussing specific trading solutions, I want to address big picture solutions. These are my own rules for trading successfully. They may not seem to address the mirror image problem, but they have worked consistently for me.

The Big Picture Solutions

1. **Pay your dues.** Success is first and foremost within your own consciousness. Do what you have to do to get to the place where success is yours internally, regardless of what is happening in the external world.

2. **Study, study, study.** I owe most of my success to the work of William O'Neil, the founder of *Investor's Business Daily*. (Thanks again, Mr. O'Neil!) Create your own library of stock market classics to study. The bibliography at the back of this book contains the best books I know on the subject.

3. **Study the major *indexes* — the Dow, the S&P 500, and the NASDAQ Composite — and learn to interpret market action and recognize major buying opportunities.** This cannot be emphasized enough. When the major indexes are in corrections or a bear market, a fantastic opportunity is presenting itself. The market always bounces back, and you must learn to recognize the next crop of new *leadership* stocks. Mr.

O'Neil's book *How to Make Money in Stocks* contains the best information I know on this subject.

4. **Take stock in the stock market; adopt a silk-share philosophy.** This approach has been invaluable to me. I'm a much better sleeper because of this philosophy! The idea is to build a portfolio of your winning stocks. When you own a stock that is doing well and you're ready to cash in and take your profits, don't! Instead, leave your profits (these are the silk shares) and let them ride. Take out your initial capital investment plus the cost of commissions, and you end up owning only those shares that represent your success. They stare you in the face every day. There are several reasons for adopting this approach:

   A. By holding onto your profits, you can see your successes every time you look at your portfolio. It's easy to get discouraged and lose confidence in the stock market, but success is contagious.

   B. If you sell out your entire position in a stock and it goes much higher, you'll feel rotten; with silk shares, you're still in the position.

   C. A group of these silk shares become like foot soldiers working on your behalf. If the silk share positions go against you, it's easier on you psychologically because they were pure profits.

   D. Holding stock positions in this way makes a statement about truly being a shareholder in a company, not just someone who is attempting to take the money and run. It creates a feeling of pride-of-ownership.

   E. Who knows what these silk shares might do for you? They might turn into really big winners or really terrible dogs. But you still have the opportunity to cash them in later if you care to.

5. **Use fundamental analysis, too.** I love technical analysis, but that doesn't mean I have blinders on in regard to fundamentals. Fundamentals are what really move the markets. I like quality companies with quality balance sheets.

6. **Look for stocks breaking out of multiple turnover formations — which is the most powerful formation.** When you see these at major buying opportunities, you're looking at big moneymakers.

Specific Trading Solutions/Suggestions

1. **Play the reversal points.** Watch a stock's price behavior when it touches the 50% or 100% lines. If support or resistance shows up in the form of a price reversal day, the upcoming direction has shown itself. In other words, if the price shows a wide range during the day with the price closing near the top or bottom of the range, the price will generally follow in the same direction.

2. **Watch for follow-through confirmation.** In subsequent days or weeks, look for the stock to follow in the direction the stock is actually going to go. Use daily and weekly charts for this purpose.

3. **Pay attention to analysts' upgrades.** If you're *bottom picking*, look for a stock that has several analysts projecting a turnaround in profits. Valid breakouts often soon follow. This is especially true of Merrill Lynch, whose picks are usually quite accurate.

4. **Follow an industry group.** If several stocks in a group are all moving above their float turnovers, the likelihood of valid breakouts is extremely good.

5. **Use other indicators for confirmation.** *MACD lines* and *stochastics* are excellent at confirming the direction the move will be taking.

6. **Consider an option strategy.** Buy a *put* and a *call option* at the same *strike price*. This *options* strategy is known as a *straddle*. It is used by traders who believe a big move in prices is about to occur but are uncertain about its direction.

7. **Study the market closely during major corrections and bear markets.** The leading stocks will bounce at their 50% or 100% turnover points. These are excellent buying opportunities.

8. **Study a stock's previous price history.** If a stock has had a long run to the upside and has already had several price reversals at the 100% level, then the likelihood for a reversal is increased.

With all of this in mind, let's discuss the most common strategies for playing the upside and the downside in the stock market.

Playing the Upside

There are four strategies for using float analysis to find winning stocks that are moving to the upside:

1. Bottom picking
2. Breakouts above strong bases of support in a rising trend
3. Playing the bounce at the 50% point
4. Playing the bounce at the 100% point

Bottom Picking

In this strategy, we track stocks that are making long down-trend price declines. The objective is to find that point in time when a solid base of support bottom is formed. The hope is that the stock will turn around and begin a long up-trend price rise. The starting point is building a list of prospective companies that are turnaround candidates. There are several approaches to building this watch list. *Investor's Business Daily* lists stocks on a **relative strength** performance basis. Every stock's price performance in the previous year is ranked on a scale of 1 to 99. The market's top performing stocks for the past year would have relative strength numbers in the 90s, and the stocks with the worst price performance are ranked with numbers between 1 and 10. If we want to find stocks that are turnaround candidates, we can

> **Bottom picking is the analysis of stocks that have been going down in price with the hope of finding one for which the price will turn around and go higher.**

begin by building a list of stocks with very low relative strength numbers. These stocks will definitely be in long down-trends.

Another approach to creating a list of potential turnaround candidates is to watch the daily list of stocks that are being upgraded or downgraded by analysts at top brokerage firms. Many brokerage houses focus on value investing and are always looking for companies that are undervalued in their opinion. By keeping an eye out for stocks that have been going down in price but are being recommended by top analysts, we can find great turnaround candidates.

The greatest plus for bottom picking is that bottom formations are extremely common. Any stock in a long-term down-trend that does turn around for a large rise to the upside will have a bottom formation and a valid breakout point. Another plus is that if you get on board a strong high flier, your profits can be sizable.

There are also several negative aspects to bottom picking. Stocks that are in long down-trends are going down for a reason. The company is having problems. It can be psychologically difficult to put your money into a company that is doing poorly. If a bottom does form and a valid breakout does occur, it will probably do so before any positive news becomes public.

Another problem with bottom picking is that when the price finally does rise above the float, it may correct downward back into the original basing area and spend plenty of time there before it actually starts heading upward. It may also be a weak base, and the price may not only correct downward, but it may just keep on going downward. A stock that has come down to, say, $6 after being at $50 may look attractive, but from $6 it can go all the way to 6 cents or lower! Then your investment is worthless.

Finding turnaround candidates with buy recommendations from several top brokerages can ease the burden, but you still aren't guaranteed success.

> **Stocks making new highs after forming a strong base are renowned for being big winners.**

Breakouts above Strong Bases of Support in a Rising Trend

This is the soundest way to buy stocks that are moving to the upside. Stocks making new highs after forming a strong base are renowned for being big winners. This is especially true for multiple float turnover formations discovered at the end of a broad market sell-off or after the first leg of a bull market. Just when the overall market looks its worst is the time that the next crop of top stocks appears to lead the market to new highs. Be especially vigilant at studying the market during market corrections and bear markets. Check the daily new-high list as the market starts tanking. The strongest companies are often the last ones to drop and the first to bounce back. Look for the stocks with the biggest bounces coming out of broad market sell-off. I know of no better place to search for breakout candidates than *Investor's Business Daily*. This newspaper has been designed to help the reader discover stocks that are breaking out above a basing pattern.

Putting your money into leading stocks with great upside potential has a psychological advantage. You'll feel more comfortable with a company with great sales and profit reports. And if you truly wait until after a major market decline to get in, you'll enjoy a long, profitable ride.

The biggest challenge in buying stocks breaking out of basing patterns is that the stock may be making its last gasp move after a long run to the upside. Strong stocks tend to have several basing patterns and breakouts before they have long price declines. If you buy a third- or fourth-tier breakout, the stock may just head lower after the breakout is over.

Buying the Bounce at the 50% Point

Stocks don't just go straight up. They have corrections to the downside, and these corrections can be buying opportunities. The true leaders in a broad market rally will often correct right at their 50% float turnover points after they have substantial moves to the upside. The trick is to know the strong companies that are basically going on sale and will bounce back strongly to the upside. You have to study and watch the market quite a bit to get a feel for this.

> The trick is to know the strong companies that are basically going on sale and will bounce back strongly to the upside.

One way to play the bounce at the 50% point is to watch the price action closely when it crosses this line. You want to see the price show plenty of strength when it reaches the 50% point. *One-day price reversals*, where the price rallies into the closing bell, can be an excellent hint that support has been found.

Obviously, if a great company's stock goes on sale, you have a fantastic buying opportunity presenting itself to you. The problem is that it is psychologically difficult to buy a stock that is moving down. You never know if some real difficulty has developed at the company and the stock is about to continue moving down in a big way.

Buying the Bounce at the 100% Point

Psychologically, the 100% float point is probably the most difficult and tricky place to buy a stock. Perhaps that's why so many stocks turn around right at this point. Here we find a stock's price dropping briefly below the float turnover, only to rally to the upside. The difficulty is that you don't know if the ownership holding the shares above the price are just going to sell into a rally or if they are going to hold tight and cause the price to rise to new high ground. You also don't know if you're looking at the beginning of a major sell-off in the stock. When a stock's price drops below the float turnover after a large rise to the upside, you may be looking at a shorting candidate and not a buying opportunity. It can be a very tough call.

> The 100% float point is probably the most difficult and tricky place to buy a stock. When a stock's price drops below the float turnover after a large rise to the upside, you may be looking at a shorting candidate and not a buying opportunity.

You can't just rely on technical analysis to buy and sell stocks. You have to do fundamental research, too. If you're convinced that the company you're looking at is sound and has a great future, step up and buy. You have to decide how much risk you're willing to take. There are so many great buying opportunities that playing the risky ones can cause your portfolio to slowly deteriorate.

Playing the Downside

Newcomers to the stock market are usually amazed to learn that money can be made when a stock is going down and not just when it goes up. The term for this is *going short* or *shorting a stock*. Going short is based on borrowing someone else's stock and then selling it in the open market with the promise that you will buy it back later and return it to its rightful owner. You are still trying to buy low and sell high. But in shorting, you sell first at a higher price and then buy it back later at a lower price. You're still buying low and selling high, but in reverse order.

Playing the downside with float analysis uses the same strategies as playing the upside, but in reverse. The strategies for using float analysis to find winning stocks that are moving to the downside are threefold:

1. Top picking or going short at the top
2. Shorting the bounce at the 50% point
3. Shorting the bounce at the 100% point

Top Picking or Going Short at the Top

Selling a stock after a long run to the upside when it breaks below its float can be very profitable. Successful topping formations, like successful bottom formations, are extremely common. If you get aboard a stock that has truly topped and is heading lower, chances are that the profits will come quite fast, since stocks generally go down faster than they go up.

As with bottom picking, the starting point strategy here is to build a list of stocks that have had great runs to the upside but are overextended and are now about to break down dramatically. Once again, a great place to build a potential list for shorting is *Investor's Business Daily*. Make a list of stocks that have great runs to the upside. These stocks have very high relative strength numbers in the 90s.

> Successful topping formations are extremely common. If you get aboard a stock that has truly topped and is heading lower, chances are that the profits will come quite fast.

Another good source for potential stocks that are topping is the big brokerage house lists of stocks that analysts are downgrading. Many top growth companies will make moves to the downside solely because an analyst lowers its rating on the stock. By keeping an eye out for stocks that have been going up in price but are now being downgraded by top analysts, we can find great shorting candidates.

The greatest plus for top picking is that topping formations are extremely common. Any stock in a long-term up-trend that does turn around for a large drop to the downside will have a top formation and a valid breakout power point. Another plus is that if you get on board a strong high flier, your profits can be sizable.

There are also several difficulties to top picking. Stocks that are in long up-trends are going up for a reason. The company is hitting on all cylinders. Shorting a company that is doing well can be psychologically difficult. And finding the point at which a stock makes its absolute top can be quite tricky. Top stocks that have done well tend to find new buyers easily on the downside because value players see a bargain when the stock's price comes down. This can easily drive the stock back up toward its previous high. This may mean that before a big drop occurs you may have to sit through a retracement to the upside while holding a losing position.

Another potential for disaster is that the stock may be only temporarily dropping below the turnover of its float. Instead of a shorting candidate, this may be a stock that is reversing at 100% of the float point and about to make a new run to the upside, forcing you to cover your short position at a big loss.

Shorting the Bounce at the 50% Point

Stocks don't just go straight down. They have retracements to the upside, and these retracements can be selling opportunities. Stocks that are in downtrends will often make retracements right at their 50% float turnover point after they have substantial moves to the downside.

One way to play the bounce at the 50% point is to watch the price action closely when it crosses this line. You hope to see the price show weakness when it crosses the 50% point. One-day price reversals where the price slumps into the closing bell can be an excellent sign that resistance has been hit.

Shorting the Retracement at the 100% Point

This also is a psychologically difficult and tricky place to sell a stock short. Here we find a stock's price rallying briefly above the float turnover only to drop dramatically to the downside. You don't know if the ownership holding the shares below the price is holding tight, thus causing the price to continue rising. You might be looking at the beginning of a major price rise in the stock. Thus, you may not be looking at a shorting candidate at all; it may turn out to have been a buying opportunity. It is very difficult to determine its category.

Final Strategies

Trading the Swings in a Sideways Market

Short-term traders will be most interested in this strategy because the buy and sell signals occur more often in a stock making a sideways move. This occurs because, in a multiple turnover sideways base, the price tends to reverse at the 50% or 100% levels several times throughout the sideways move. I have noticed that this strategy works best on leading stocks that have large floats and fairly rapid turnovers. I believe the reason is that leading stocks such as Intel have plenty of support from *institutional players*. Thus, when their prices start to go sideways, they tend to form a base of support for the next big rise in prices.

The Look of a Strong Base of Support

Strong bases of support are recognized through experience. Study the charts in the text as well as those presented in appendix A. As a general rule, a strong base is one in which the price range is not too wide. Usually it will have large volume spikes on the far left and near the top of the float turnover followed by small volume on the right. If the price range is wide and the larger volume spikes are near the bottom, then breakouts tend to lack power. This is because the large volume ownership at the bottom of the float turnover will sell into the breakout, causing resistance to further upside movement.

Tracking Large Numbers of Stocks and What It Tells You

A fascinating aspect of float analysis is the information you can get from tracking large numbers of stocks. My present system can scan a thousand stocks. From this analysis comes the observation that bull markets end when the number of stocks breaking above the turnover of their floats decreases while the number of stocks breaking below the turnover of their floats increases. The same phenomenon occurs in reverse at the end of broad market corrections or bear markets. The number of stocks breaking above their floats will begin to increase and the number breaking below their floats will start to decrease. I have seen this occur on several occasions. In the bear market of 1998, the number of stocks breaking above their floats dwindled down to zero while the number of stocks moving below their floats increased dramatically. As the new bull market began, the reverse began to occur. Stocks began to break above their floats while the number of stocks breaking below their floats decreased dramatically.

Tracking Industry Groups

Another way of tracking large numbers of stocks is to track them by *industry group*. Stocks within groups tend to move together. When they all start to break out above their floats, it is a sure sign that the whole group is heading higher. This has happened twice to the semiconductor industry in the nine years that I have studied the market.

> **Float analysis looks at stocks in the most elementary and holistic of ways. It defines quantitatively the dimensions of a bottom and a top. It expands the definition of support and resistance. Plus, float analysis creates a new model of stock behavior by demonstrating recurring float turnover formations.**

Tracking Indexes

Many people have asked me about using float analysis to track indexes. As of the writing of this book, I have yet to try this. A stock's float is a very specific number for each individual stock, so it would seem that an index would not be as valid as it is for individual stocks. This may be a subject for future study.

Summary

Float analysis is an important new field of study in technical stock research for a number of reasons. First, it looks at stocks in the most elementary and holistic of ways. A stock has only three components when it is trading — the float, the price, and the volume of shares traded. Traditional price and volume charts show only two-thirds of a stock's true picture. The float is the missing third. Second, it defines quantitatively the dimensions of a bottom and a top. A bottom will always be the lowest float turnover with a breakout buy point in a stock's trading history. A top will always be the highest float turnover with a breakout sell point in a stock's trading history. Third, it expands the definition of support and resistance. Support, then, is having the float turnover below the price. Resistance is having the float turnover above the price. In special-case situations, float analysis demonstrates overhead support in which the float turnover is briefly above the price and resistance below in which the float turnover is briefly below the price. Finally, float analysis creates a new model of stock behavior by demonstrating recurring float turnover formations. It creates a model with which one can analyze any stock. This model is a tool to make money by helping investors be more informed when it comes to buying and selling stock.

APPENDIX A

A Compendium of Float Analysis Formations

W hat follows is 100 float turnover examples — 10 examples for each of the 10 discoveries covered in chapter 2. This appendix is for the serious student of float analysis who will want to study as many formation examples as possible. It is also an attempt to show that I did not find examples just to fit my ideas. Float turnover formations are commonplace, and the following collection of examples will hopefully help convince any skeptical reader. Some day, tracking float turnovers will be as commonplace as tracking the moving average. This will occur when technicians realize that all stocks always trade in relation to their floating supply of shares and that float analysis is one way to see this relationship.

DISCOVERY 1

The Multiple Float Turnover
Base of Support Formation

Multiple float turnover formations are the strongest
bases of support.

Examples:

A-1　　Ameritrade (AMTD)
A-2　　Amazon.com (AMZN)
A-3　　CMGI Information Svcs. (CMGI)
A-4　　Doubleclick Inc. (DCLK)
A-5　　Ebay Inc. (EBAY)
A-6　　Go2Net Inc. (GNET)
A-7　　Knight/Trimark (NITE)
A-8　　Internet Capital Group (ICGE)
A-9　　Infospace (INSP)
A-10　　Commerce One Inc. (CMRC)

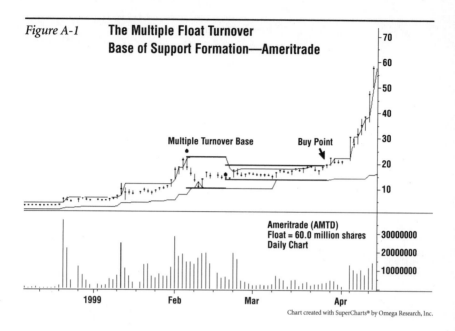

Figure A-1

The Multiple Float Turnover Base of Support Formation—Ameritrade

Multiple Turnover Base

Buy Point

Ameritrade (AMTD)
Float = 60.0 million shares
Daily Chart

1999   Feb   Mar   Apr

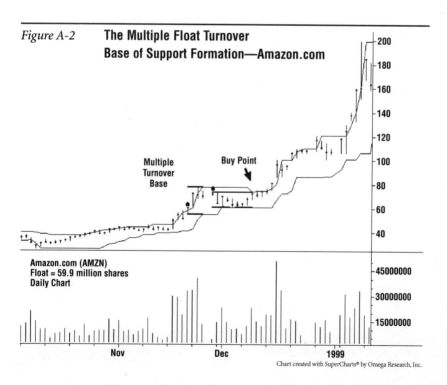

Figure A-2

The Multiple Float Turnover Base of Support Formation—Amazon.com

Multiple
Turnover
Base

Buy Point

Amazon.com (AMZN)
Float = 59.9 million shares
Daily Chart

Nov   Dec   1999

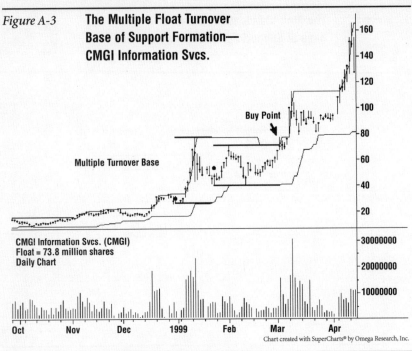

Figure A-3

The Multiple Float Turnover Base of Support Formation— CMGI Information Svcs.

Buy Point

Multiple Turnover Base

CMGI Information Svcs. (CMGI)
Float = 73.8 million shares
Daily Chart

Chart created with SuperCharts® by Omega Research, Inc.

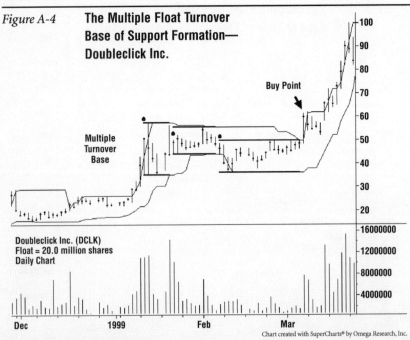

Figure A-4

The Multiple Float Turnover Base of Support Formation— Doubleclick Inc.

Buy Point

Multiple
Turnover
Base

Doubleclick Inc. (DCLK)
Float = 20.0 million shares
Daily Chart

Chart created with SuperCharts® by Omega Research, Inc.

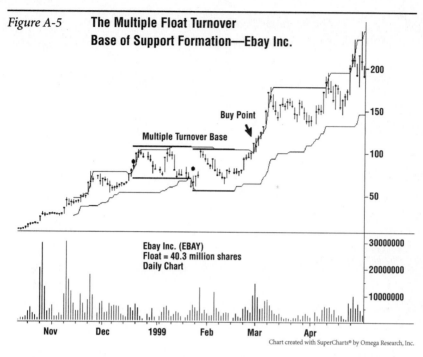

Figure A-5 **The Multiple Float Turnover
Base of Support Formation—Ebay Inc.**

Buy Point

Multiple Turnover Base

Ebay Inc. (EBAY)
Float = 40.3 million shares
Daily Chart

200

150

100

50

30000000

20000000

10000000

Nov   Dec   1999   Feb   Mar   Apr

Chart created with SuperCharts® by Omega Research, Inc.

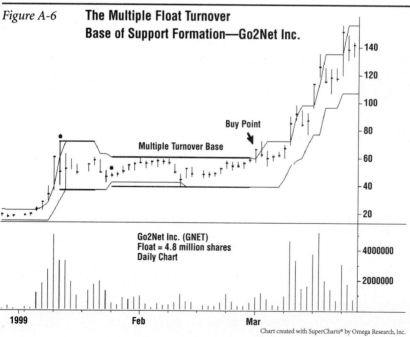

Figure A-6 **The Multiple Float Turnover
Base of Support Formation—Go2Net Inc.**

Buy Point

Multiple Turnover Base

Go2Net Inc. (GNET)
Float = 4.8 million shares
Daily Chart

140

120

100

80

60

40

20

4000000

2000000

1999   Feb   Mar

Chart created with SuperCharts® by Omega Research, Inc.

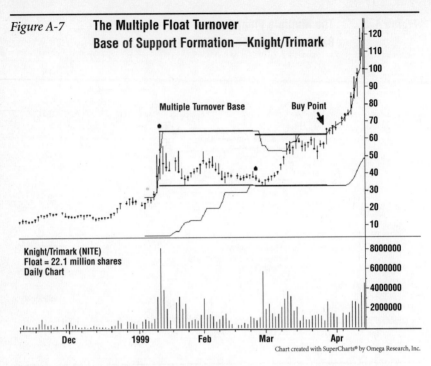

Figure A-7 **The Multiple Float Turnover Base of Support Formation—Knight/Trimark**

Multiple Turnover Base

Buy Point

Knight/Trimark (NITE)
Float = 22.1 million shares
Daily Chart

Chart created with SuperCharts® by Omega Research, Inc.

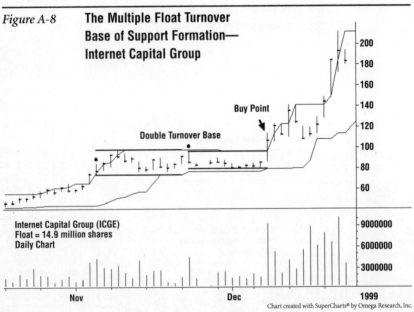

Figure A-8 **The Multiple Float Turnover Base of Support Formation— Internet Capital Group**

Buy Point

Double Turnover Base

Internet Capital Group (ICGE)
Float = 14.9 million shares
Daily Chart

Chart created with SuperCharts® by Omega Research, Inc.

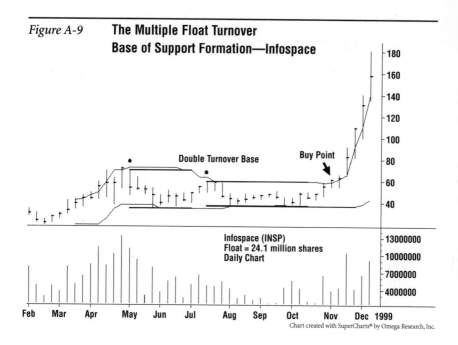

Figure A-9 **The Multiple Float Turnover Base of Support Formation—Infospace**

Double Turnover Base

Buy Point

Infospace (INSP)
Float = 24.1 million shares
Daily Chart

Chart created with SuperCharts® by Omega Research, Inc.

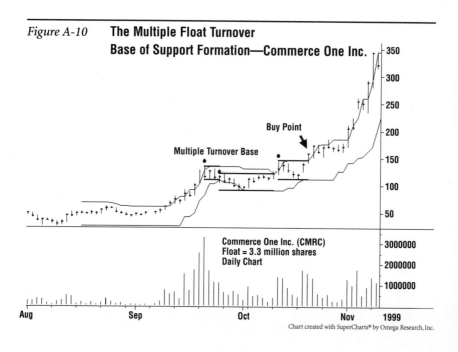

Figure A-10 **The Multiple Float Turnover Base of Support Formation—Commerce One Inc.**

Buy Point

Multiple Turnover Base

Commerce One Inc. (CMRC)
Float = 3.3 million shares
Daily Chart

Chart created with SuperCharts® by Omega Research, Inc.

DISCOVERY 2

The Turnover at a Bottom

Single float turnover formations with a breakout buy point always occur at absolute bottoms and are also found at intermediate bottoms.

Examples:

A-11   Advanced Micro Devices (AMD)
A-12   Banyan Systems (BNYN)
A-13   Cognex Inc. (CGNX)
A-14   Conseco Inc. (CNC)
A-15   Genesco Inc. (GCO)
A-16   LCC Intl. Inc. (LCCI)
A-17   Nature's Bounty Inc. (NBTY)
A-18   Novell Inc. (NOVL)
A-19   Recoton Corp. (RCOT)
A-20   Softech Inc. (SOFT)

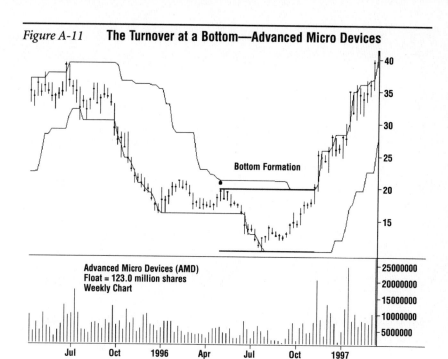

Figure A-11   **The Turnover at a Bottom—Advanced Micro Devices**

Bottom Formation

Advanced Micro Devices (AMD)
Float = 123.0 million shares
Weekly Chart

Chart created with SuperCharts® by Omega Research, Inc.

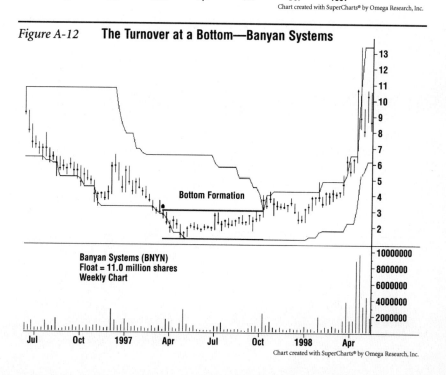

Figure A-12   **The Turnover at a Bottom—Banyan Systems**

Bottom Formation

Banyan Systems (BNYN)
Float = 11.0 million shares
Weekly Chart

Chart created with SuperCharts® by Omega Research, Inc.

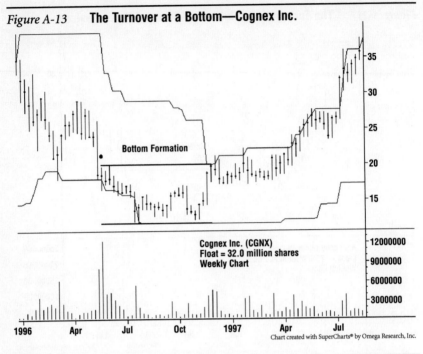

Figure A-13 **The Turnover at a Bottom—Cognex Inc.**

Bottom Formation

Cognex Inc. (CGNX)
Float = 32.0 million shares
Weekly Chart

Chart created with SuperCharts® by Omega Research, Inc.

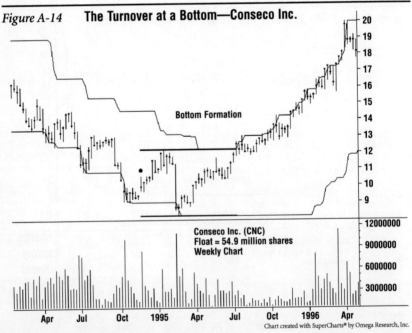

Figure A-14 **The Turnover at a Bottom—Conseco Inc.**

Bottom Formation

Conseco Inc. (CNC)
Float = 54.9 million shares
Weekly Chart

Chart created with SuperCharts® by Omega Research, Inc.

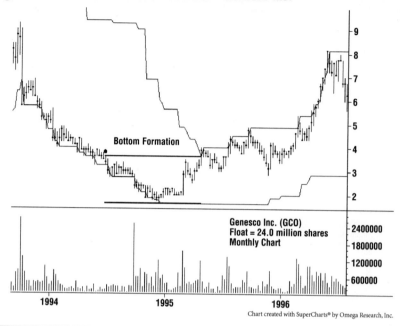

Figure A-15 **The Turnover at a Bottom—Genesco Inc.**

Bottom Formation

Genesco Inc. (GCO)
Float = 24.0 million shares
Monthly Chart

Chart created with SuperCharts® by Omega Research, Inc.

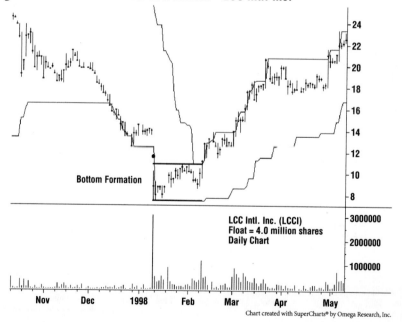

Figure A-16 **The Turnover at a Bottom—LCC Intl. Inc.**

Bottom Formation

LCC Intl. Inc. (LCCI)
Float = 4.0 million shares
Daily Chart

Chart created with SuperCharts® by Omega Research, Inc.

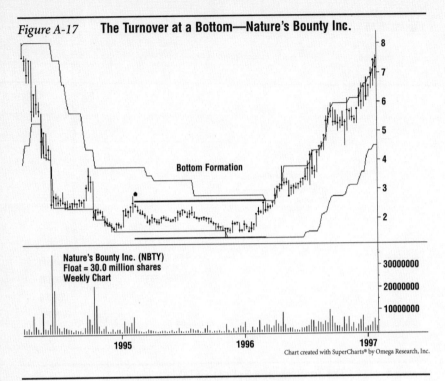

Figure A-17   **The Turnover at a Bottom—Nature's Bounty Inc.**

Bottom Formation

Nature's Bounty Inc. (NBTY)
Float = 30.0 million shares
Weekly Chart

30000000
20000000
10000000

1995   1996   1997

Chart created with SuperCharts® by Omega Research, Inc.

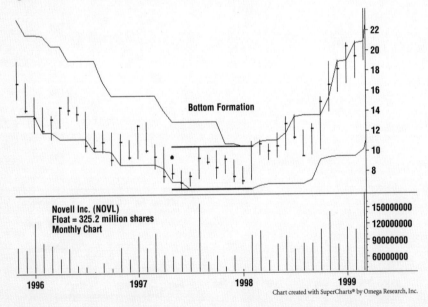

Figure A-18   **The Turnover at a Bottom—Novell Inc.**

Bottom Formation

Novell Inc. (NOVL)
Float = 325.2 million shares
Monthly Chart

150000000
120000000
90000000
60000000

1996   1997   1998   1999

Chart created with SuperCharts® by Omega Research, Inc.

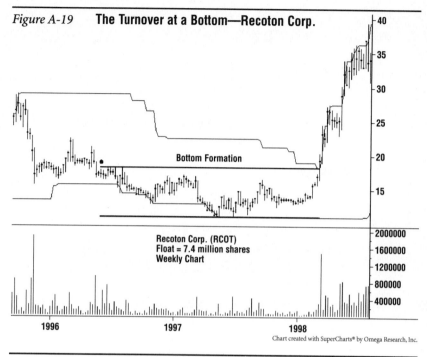

Figure A-19 **The Turnover at a Bottom—Recoton Corp.**

Bottom Formation

Recoton Corp. (RCOT)
Float = 7.4 million shares
Weekly Chart

1996   1997   1998

Chart created with SuperCharts® by Omega Research, Inc.

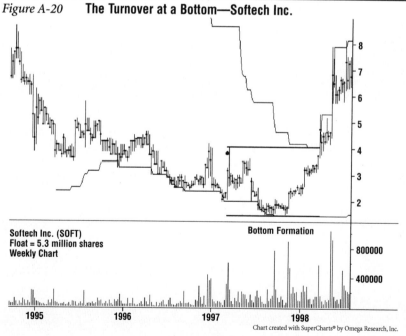

Figure A-20 **The Turnover at a Bottom—Softech Inc.**

Bottom Formation

Softech Inc. (SOFT)
Float = 5.3 million shares
Weekly Chart

1995   1996   1997   1998

Chart created with SuperCharts® by Omega Research, Inc.

DISCOVERY 3

The Top Formation

Single float turnover formations with a breakout sell point always occur at absolute tops and are also found at intermediate tops.

Examples:

A-21	American Technical Ceramics (AMK)
A-22	American Bingo & Gaming (BNGO)
A-23	Cyprus Semiconductor (CY)
A-24	4 Kids Entertainment (KIDE)
A-25	Kulicke & Soffa Ind. (KLIC)
A-26	Lam Research (LRCX)
A-27	Novellus Systems Inc. (NVLS)
A-28	Petsmart Inc. (PETM)
A-29	Rational Software (RATL)
A-30	Three Com Corp. (COMS)

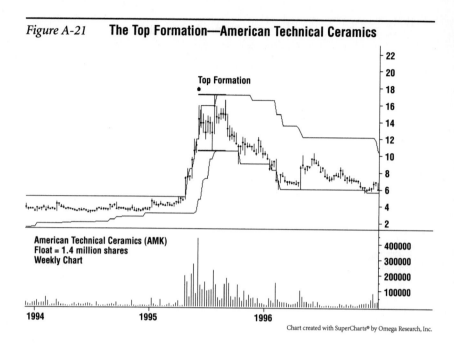

Figure A-21   The Top Formation—American Technical Ceramics

Top Formation

American Technical Ceramics (AMK)
Float = 1.4 million shares
Weekly Chart

1994   1995   1996

Chart created with SuperCharts® by Omega Research, Inc.

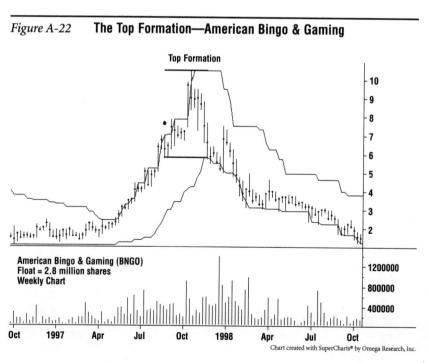

Figure A-22   The Top Formation—American Bingo & Gaming

Top Formation

American Bingo & Gaming (BNGO)
Float = 2.8 million shares
Weekly Chart

Oct   1997   Apr   Jul   Oct   1998   Apr   Jul   Oct

Chart created with SuperCharts® by Omega Research, Inc.

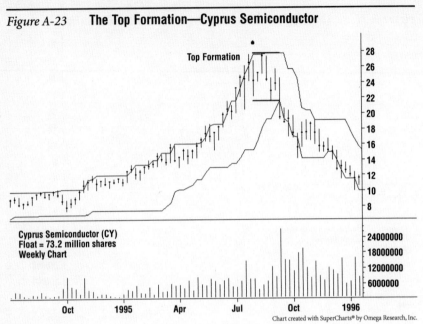

Figure A-23 **The Top Formation—Cyprus Semiconductor**

Top Formation

Cyprus Semiconductor (CY)
Float = 73.2 million shares
Weekly Chart

Chart created with SuperCharts® by Omega Research, Inc.

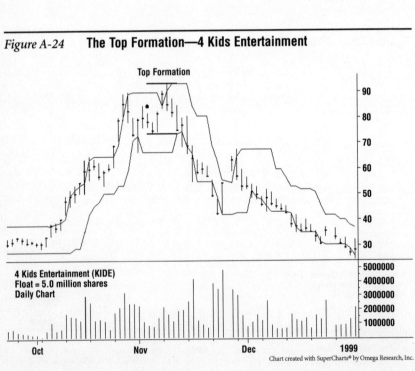

Figure A-24 **The Top Formation—4 Kids Entertainment**

Top Formation

4 Kids Entertainment (KIDE)
Float = 5.0 million shares
Daily Chart

Chart created with SuperCharts® by Omega Research, Inc.

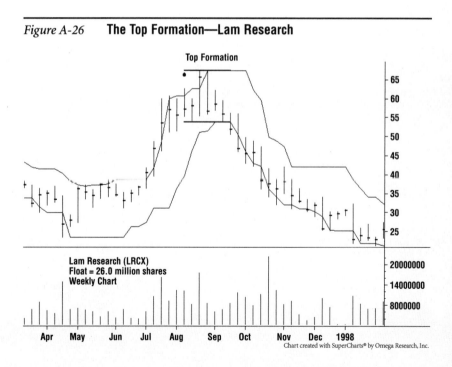

Figure A-25 **The Top Formation—Kulicke & Soffa Ind.**

Top Formation

55
50
45
40
35
30
25
20
15
10

Kulicke & Soffa Ind. (KLIC)
Float = 22.3 million shares
Weekly Chart

16000000
12000000
8000000
4000000

Nov Dec 1997 Feb Mar Apr May Jun Jul Aug Sep Oct Nov Dec 1998

Chart created with SuperCharts® by Omega Research, Inc.

Figure A-26 **The Top Formation—Lam Research**

Top Formation

65
60
55
50
45
40
35
30
25

Lam Research (LRCX)
Float = 26.0 million shares
Weekly Chart

20000000
14000000
8000000

Apr May Jun Jul Aug Sep Oct Nov Dec 1998

Chart created with SuperCharts® by Omega Research, Inc.

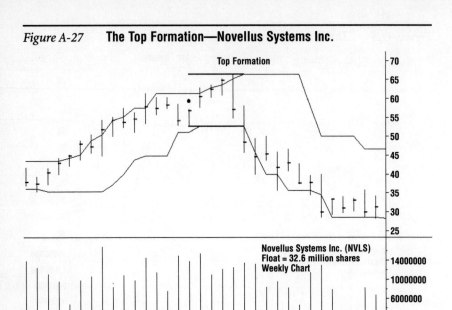

Figure A-27   **The Top Formation—Novellus Systems Inc.**

Top Formation

Novellus Systems Inc. (NVLS)
Float = 32.6 million shares
Weekly Chart

Chart created with SuperCharts® by Omega Research, Inc.

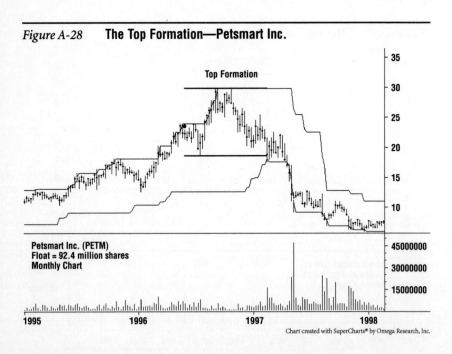

Figure A-28   **The Top Formation—Petsmart Inc.**

Top Formation

Petsmart Inc. (PETM)
Float = 92.4 million shares
Monthly Chart

Chart created with SuperCharts® by Omega Research, Inc.

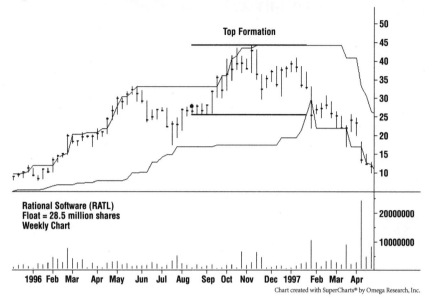

Figure A-29   **The Top Formation—Rational Software**

Top Formation

Rational Software (RATL)
Float = 28.5 million shares
Weekly Chart

1996 Feb Mar Apr May Jun Jul Aug Sep Oct Nov Dec 1997 Feb Mar Apr

Chart created with SuperCharts® by Omega Research, Inc.

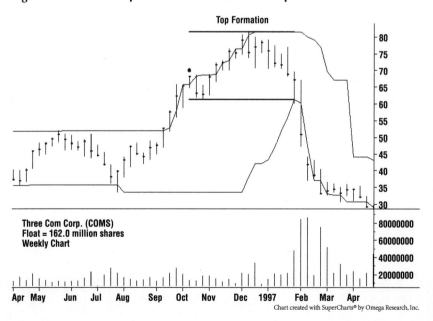

Figure A-30   **The Top Formation—Three Com Corp.**

Top Formation

Three Com Corp. (COMS)
Float = 162.0 million shares
Weekly Chart

Apr May Jun Jul Aug Sep Oct Nov Dec 1997 Feb Mar Apr

Chart created with SuperCharts® by Omega Research, Inc.

DISCOVERY 4

The Base of Support within a Correction Formation

Single float turnover formations with a breakout buy point occur at the bottom of price corrections.

Examples:

A-31   Action Performance (ACTN)
A-32   Adaptec Inc. (ADPT)
A-33   CMG Information (CMGI)
A-34   Excite (XCIT)
A-35   Go2Net Inc. (GNET)
A-36   Merck & Co. Inc. (MRK)
A-37   Mindspring Enterprise (MSPG)
A-38   Photronics Inc. (PLAB)
A-39   PSI Net Inc. (PSIX)
A-40   Vitesse Semiconductor (VTSS)

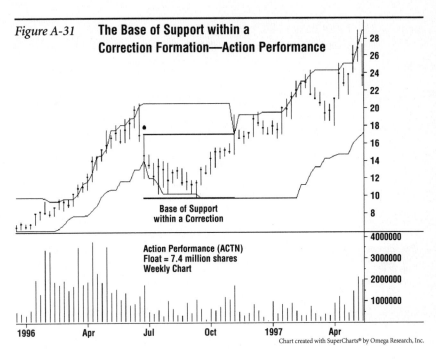

Figure A-31

The Base of Support within a Correction Formation—Action Performance

Base of Support within a Correction

Action Performance (ACTN)
Float = 7.4 million shares
Weekly Chart

Chart created with SuperCharts® by Omega Research, Inc.

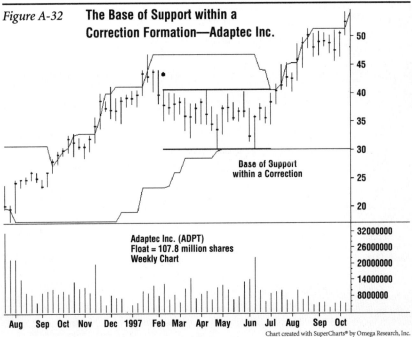

Figure A-32

The Base of Support within a Correction Formation—Adaptec Inc.

Base of Support within a Correction

Adaptec Inc. (ADPT)
Float = 107.8 million shares
Weekly Chart

Chart created with SuperCharts® by Omega Research, Inc.

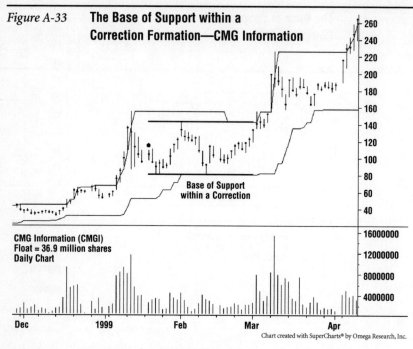

Figure A-33

The Base of Support within a Correction Formation—CMG Information

Base of Support
within a Correction

CMG Information (CMGI)
Float = 36.9 million shares
Daily Chart

Dec   1999   Feb   Mar   Apr

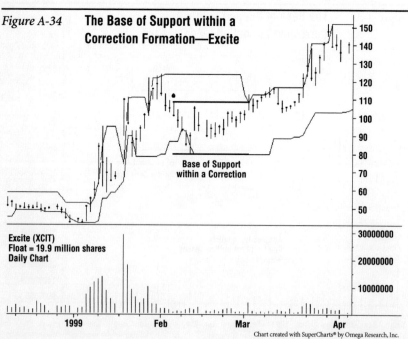

Figure A-34

The Base of Support within a Correction Formation—Excite

Base of Support
within a Correction

Excite (XCIT)
Float = 19.9 million shares
Daily Chart

1999   Feb   Mar   Apr

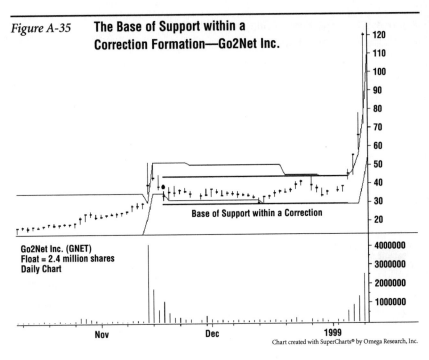

Figure A-35   **The Base of Support within a Correction Formation—Go2Net Inc.**

Base of Support within a Correction

Go2Net Inc. (GNET)
Float = 2.4 million shares
Daily Chart

Nov   Dec   1999

Chart created with SuperCharts® by Omega Research, Inc.

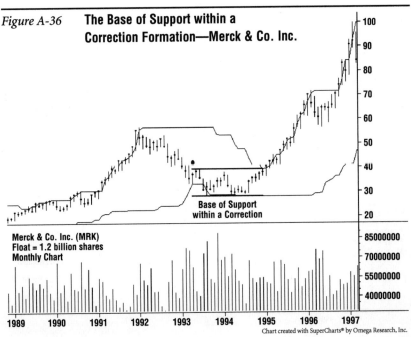

Figure A-36   **The Base of Support within a Correction Formation—Merck & Co. Inc.**

Base of Support
within a Correction

Merck & Co. Inc. (MRK)
Float = 1.2 billion shares
Monthly Chart

1989   1990   1991   1992   1993   1994   1995   1996   1997

Chart created with SuperCharts® by Omega Research, Inc.

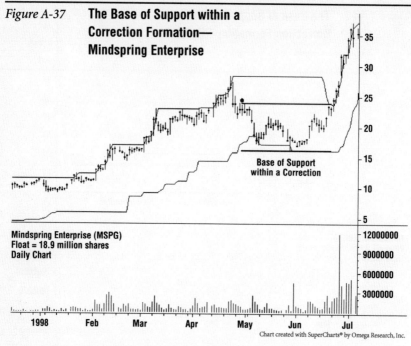

Figure A-37 **The Base of Support within a Correction Formation— Mindspring Enterprise**

Base of Support
within a Correction

Mindspring Enterprise (MSPG)
Float = 18.9 million shares
Daily Chart

Chart created with SuperCharts® by Omega Research, Inc.

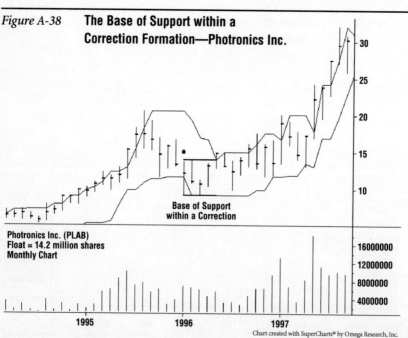

Figure A-38 **The Base of Support within a Correction Formation—Photronics Inc.**

Base of Support
within a Correction

Photronics Inc. (PLAB)
Float = 14.2 million shares
Monthly Chart

Chart created with SuperCharts® by Omega Research, Inc.

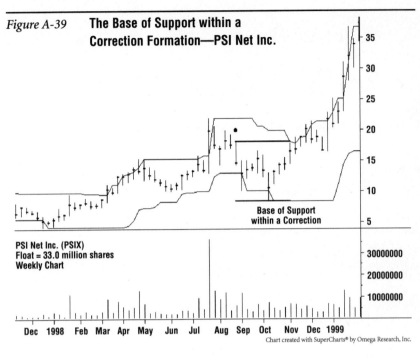

Figure A-39 **The Base of Support within a Correction Formation—PSI Net Inc.**

Base of Support
within a Correction

PSI Net Inc. (PSIX)
Float = 33.0 million shares
Weekly Chart

Chart created with SuperCharts® by Omega Research, Inc.

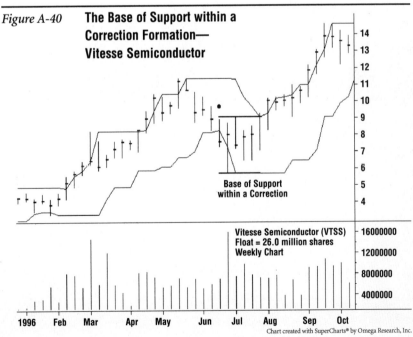

Figure A-40 **The Base of Support within a Correction Formation— Vitesse Semiconductor**

Base of Support
within a Correction

Vitesse Semiconductor (VTSS)
Float = 26.0 million shares
Weekly Chart

Chart created with SuperCharts® by Omega Research, Inc.

DISCOVERY 5

The Base of Support in a Rising Trend Formation

Single float turnover formations with a breakout buy point occur at price consolidation basing areas in uptrends.

Examples:

A-41   Analytical Surveys (ANLT)
A-42   Commerce One Inc. (CMRC)
A-43   Dataram Inc. (DTM)
A-44   Elcom (ELCO)
A-45   General Magic (GMGC)
A-46   Metricom (MCOM)
A-47   Mindspring Enterprise (MSPG)
A-48   Silicon Storage (SSTI)
A-49   Wet Seal Inc. (WTSLA)
A-50   Xcelera (XLA) [previously known as
        Scandinavia (SCF)]

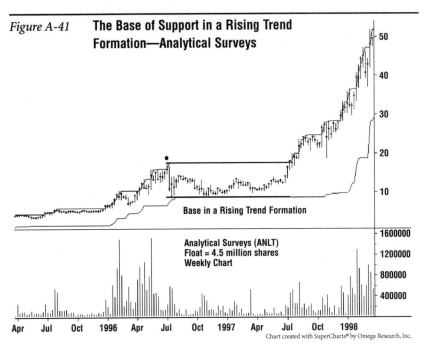

Figure A-41 **The Base of Support in a Rising Trend Formation—Analytical Surveys**

Base in a Rising Trend Formation

Analytical Surveys (ANLT)
Float = 4.5 million shares
Weekly Chart

Chart created with SuperCharts® by Omega Research, Inc.

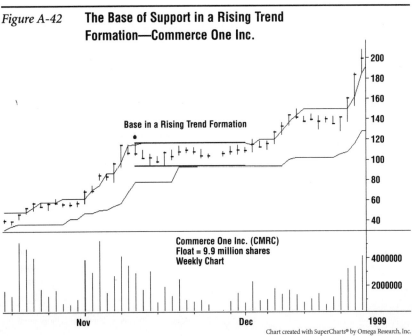

Figure A-42 **The Base of Support in a Rising Trend Formation—Commerce One Inc.**

Base in a Rising Trend Formation

Commerce One Inc. (CMRC)
Float = 9.9 million shares
Weekly Chart

Chart created with SuperCharts® by Omega Research, Inc.

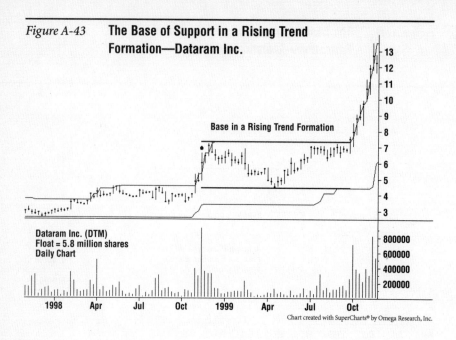

Figure A-43 **The Base of Support in a Rising Trend Formation—Dataram Inc.**

Base in a Rising Trend Formation

Dataram Inc. (DTM)
Float = 5.8 million shares
Daily Chart

Chart created with SuperCharts® by Omega Research, Inc.

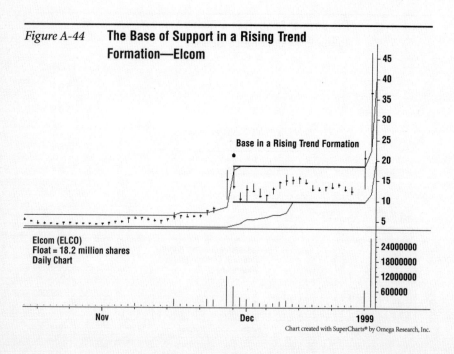

Figure A-44 **The Base of Support in a Rising Trend Formation—Elcom**

Base in a Rising Trend Formation

Elcom (ELCO)
Float = 18.2 million shares
Daily Chart

Chart created with SuperCharts® by Omega Research, Inc.

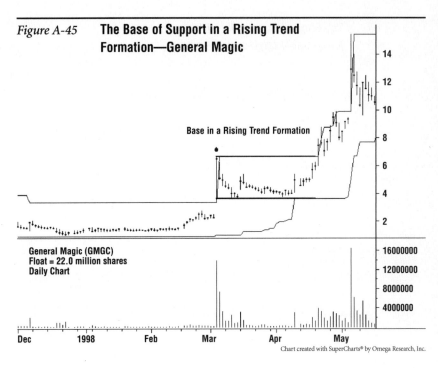

Figure A-45 **The Base of Support in a Rising Trend
Formation—General Magic**

Base in a Rising Trend Formation

General Magic (GMGC)
Float = 22.0 million shares
Daily Chart

Chart created with SuperCharts® by Omega Research, Inc.

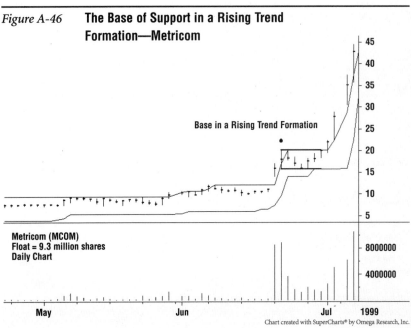

Figure A-46 **The Base of Support in a Rising Trend
Formation—Metricom**

Base in a Rising Trend Formation

Metricom (MCOM)
Float = 9.3 million shares
Daily Chart

Chart created with SuperCharts® by Omega Research, Inc.

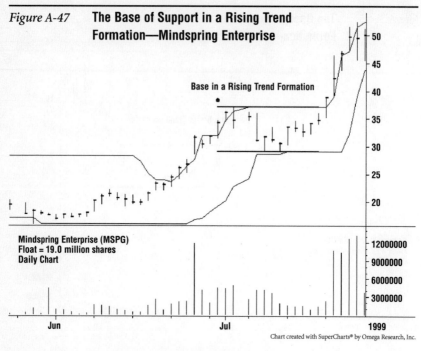

Figure A-47 **The Base of Support in a Rising Trend Formation—Mindspring Enterprise**

Base in a Rising Trend Formation

Mindspring Enterprise (MSPG)
Float = 19.0 million shares
Daily Chart

Chart created with SuperCharts® by Omega Research, Inc.

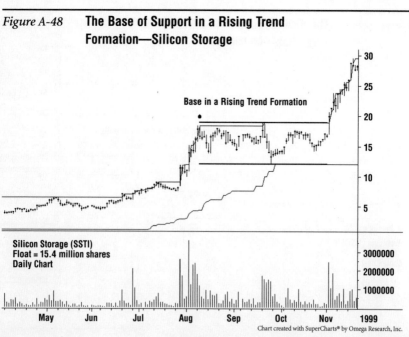

Figure A-48 **The Base of Support in a Rising Trend Formation—Silicon Storage**

Base in a Rising Trend Formation

Silicon Storage (SSTI)
Float = 15.4 million shares
Daily Chart

Chart created with SuperCharts® by Omega Research, Inc.

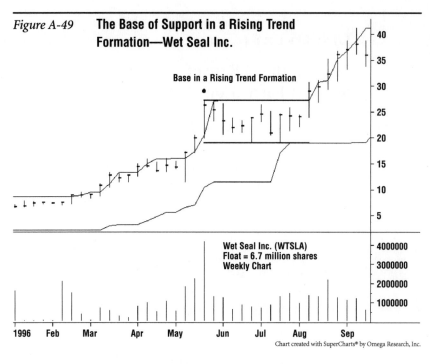

Figure A-49 **The Base of Support in a Rising Trend Formation—Wet Seal Inc.**

Base in a Rising Trend Formation

Wet Seal Inc. (WTSLA)
Float = 6.7 million shares
Weekly Chart

Chart created with SuperCharts® by Omega Research, Inc.

Figure A-50 **The Base of Support in a Rising Trend Formation—Xcelera**

Base in a Rising Trend Formation

Xcelera (XLA) [previously known as Scandinavia (SCF)]
Float = 3.0 million shares
Daily Chart

Chart created with SuperCharts® by Omega Research, Inc.

DISCOVERY 6

The Overhead Base of Support Formation

Price support in up-trends occurs as a stock's price falls below the float turnover price range, thus giving rise to a single float turnover overhead support formation with a breakout to the downside buy point.

Examples:

A-51   ADC Telecommunications (ADCT)

A-52   Amgen Inc. (AMGN)

A-53   Best Buy Co. Inc. (BBY)

A-54   Chico's FAS Inc. (CHCS)

A-55   Dell Computer Corp. (DELL)

A-56   Globalstar Telecom (GSTRF)

A-57   KLA Tencor (KLAC)

A-58   Network Appliance (NTAP)

A-59   Northern Trust Corp. (NTRS)

A-60   Paychex Inc. (PAYX)

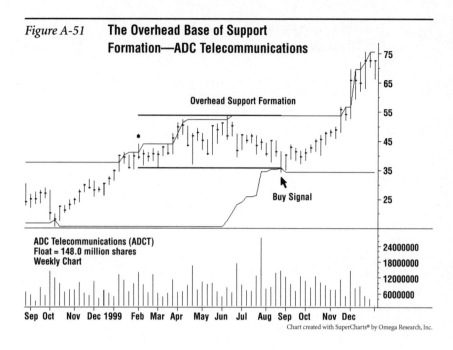

Figure A-51 **The Overhead Base of Support Formation—ADC Telecommunications**

Overhead Support Formation

Buy Signal

ADC Telecommunications (ADCT)
Float = 148.0 million shares
Weekly Chart

Sep Oct   Nov   Dec 1999   Feb   Mar   Apr   May   Jun   Jul   Aug   Sep   Oct   Nov   Dec

Chart created with SuperCharts® by Omega Research, Inc.

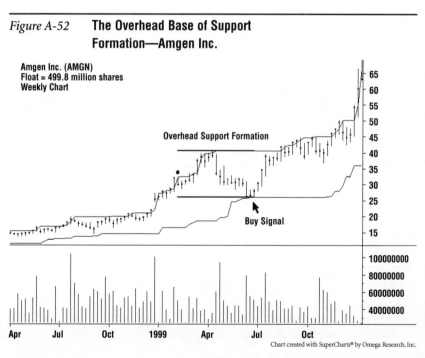

Figure A-52 **The Overhead Base of Support Formation—Amgen Inc.**

Amgen Inc. (AMGN)
Float = 499.8 million shares
Weekly Chart

Overhead Support Formation

Buy Signal

Apr   Jul   Oct   1999   Apr   Jul   Oct

Chart created with SuperCharts® by Omega Research, Inc.

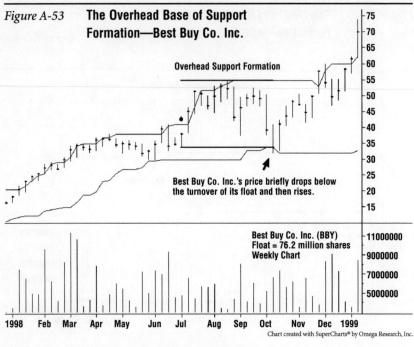

Figure A-53 **The Overhead Base of Support Formation—Best Buy Co. Inc.**

Overhead Support Formation

Best Buy Co. Inc.'s price briefly drops below the turnover of its float and then rises.

Best Buy Co. Inc. (BBY)
Float = 76.2 million shares
Weekly Chart

Chart created with SuperCharts® by Omega Research, Inc.

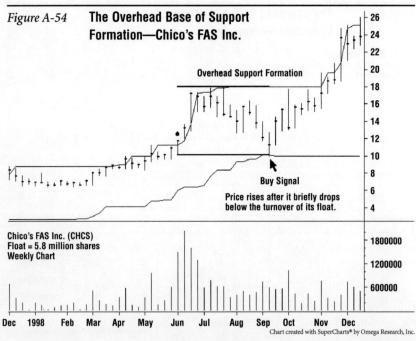

Figure A-54 **The Overhead Base of Support Formation—Chico's FAS Inc.**

Overhead Support Formation

Buy Signal

Price rises after it briefly drops below the turnover of its float.

Chico's FAS Inc. (CHCS)
Float = 5.8 million shares
Weekly Chart

Chart created with SuperCharts® by Omega Research, Inc.

Figure A-55   **The Overhead Base of Support
Formation—Dell Computer Corp.**

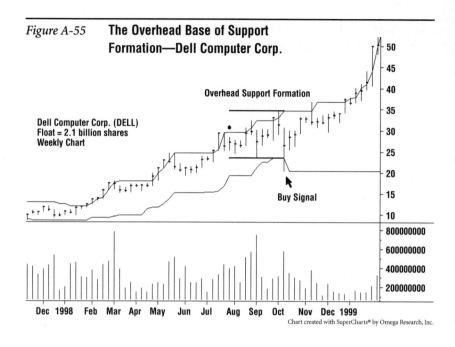

Overhead Support Formation

Dell Computer Corp. (DELL)
Float = 2.1 billion shares
Weekly Chart

Buy Signal

50
45
40
35
30
25
20
15
10

800000000
600000000
400000000
200000000

Dec 1998 Feb Mar Apr May Jun Jul Aug Sep Oct Nov Dec 1999

Chart created with SuperCharts® by Omega Research, Inc.

Figure A-56   **The Overhead Base of Support
Formation—Globalstar Telecom**

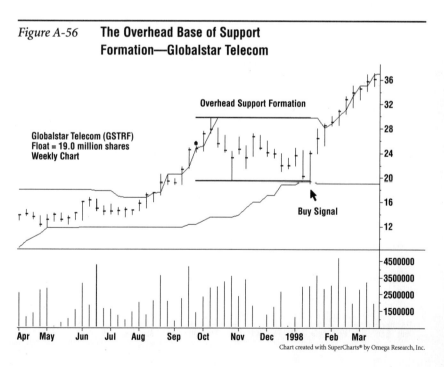

Overhead Support Formation

Globalstar Telecom (GSTRF)
Float = 19.0 million shares
Weekly Chart

Buy Signal

36
32
28
24
20
16
12

4500000
3500000
2500000
1500000

Apr May Jun Jul Aug Sep Oct Nov Dec 1998 Feb Mar

Chart created with SuperCharts® by Omega Research, Inc.

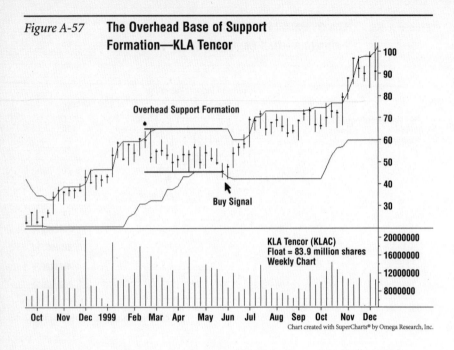

Figure A-57   **The Overhead Base of Support Formation—KLA Tencor**

Overhead Support Formation

Buy Signal

KLA Tencor (KLAC)
Float = 83.9 million shares
Weekly Chart

Oct   Nov   Dec   1999   Feb   Mar   Apr   May   Jun   Jul   Aug   Sep   Oct   Nov   Dec

Chart created with SuperCharts® by Omega Research, Inc.

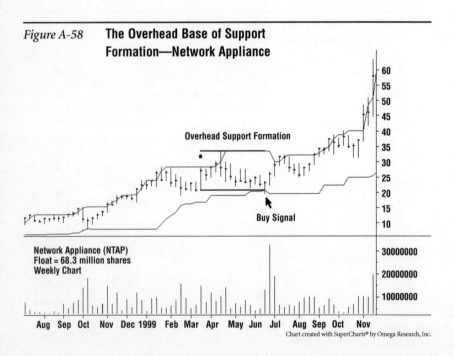

Figure A-58   **The Overhead Base of Support Formation—Network Appliance**

Overhead Support Formation

Buy Signal

Network Appliance (NTAP)
Float = 68.3 million shares
Weekly Chart

Aug   Sep   Oct   Nov   Dec   1999   Feb   Mar   Apr   May   Jun   Jul   Aug   Sep   Oct   Nov

Chart created with SuperCharts® by Omega Research, Inc.

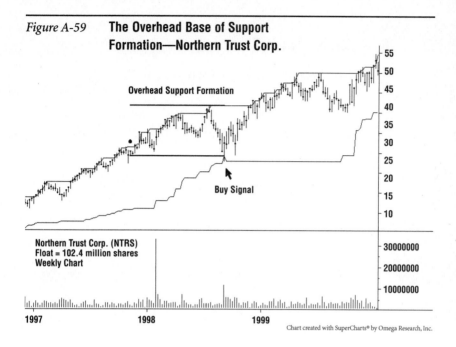

Figure A-59 **The Overhead Base of Support Formation—Northern Trust Corp.**

Overhead Support Formation

Buy Signal

Northern Trust Corp. (NTRS)
Float = 102.4 million shares
Weekly Chart

Chart created with SuperCharts® by Omega Research, Inc.

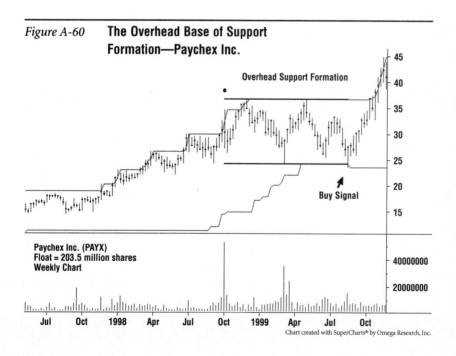

Figure A-60 **The Overhead Base of Support Formation—Paychex Inc.**

Overhead Support Formation

Buy Signal

Paychex Inc. (PAYX)
Float = 203.5 million shares
Weekly Chart

Chart created with SuperCharts® by Omega Research, Inc.

DISCOVERY 7

The Extension Formation

Single float turnover formations with a sell point occur in price extensions both slow and fast.

Examples:

A-61   Adaptec Inc. (ADPT)
A-62   Dell Computer Corp. (DELL)
A-63   Intel Corp. (INTC)
A-64   Coca Cola (KO)
A-65   McDonald's Corp. (MCD)
A-66   Microsoft Corp. (MSFT)
A-67   Thermotrex Corp. (TKN)
A-68   Online Systems Services Inc. (WEBB)
A-69   Wal-Mart Stores (WMT)
A-70   Exxon Corp. (XON)

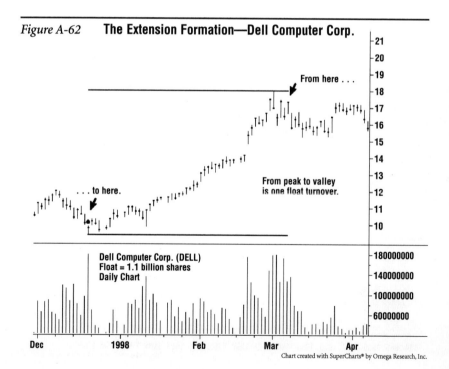

Figure A-61   **The Extension Formation—Adaptec Inc.**

Two price extensions that
are one turnover in length

Adaptec Inc. (ADPT)
Float = 107.8 million shares
Weekly Chart

1996   1997   1998

Chart created with SuperCharts® by Omega Research, Inc.

Figure A-62   **The Extension Formation—Dell Computer Corp.**

From here . . .

. . . to here.

From peak to valley
is one float turnover.

Dell Computer Corp. (DELL)
Float = 1.1 billion shares
Daily Chart

Dec   1998   Feb   Mar   Apr

Chart created with SuperCharts® by Omega Research, Inc.

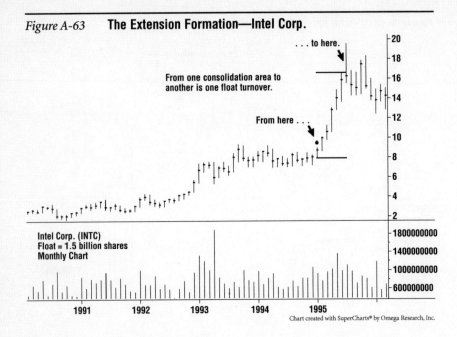

Figure A-63 **The Extension Formation—Intel Corp.**

. . . to here.

From one consolidation area to
another is one float turnover.

From here . . .

Intel Corp. (INTC)
Float = 1.5 billion shares
Monthly Chart

1991   1992   1993   1994   1995

Chart created with SuperCharts® by Omega Research, Inc.

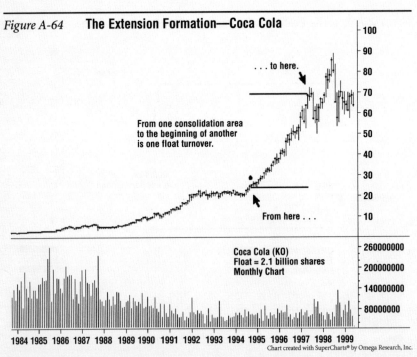

Figure A-64 **The Extension Formation—Coca Cola**

. . . to here.

From one consolidation area
to the beginning of another
is one float turnover.

From here . . .

Coca Cola (KO)
Float = 2.1 billion shares
Monthly Chart

1984 1985 1986 1987 1988 1989 1990 1991 1992 1993 1994 1995 1996 1997 1998 1999

Chart created with SuperCharts® by Omega Research, Inc.

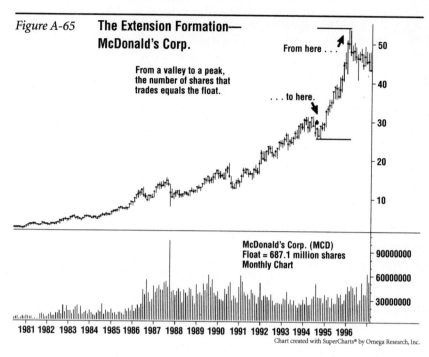

Figure A-65

The Extension Formation—McDonald's Corp.

From here . . .

From a valley to a peak,
the number of shares that
trades equals the float.

. . . to here.

McDonald's Corp. (MCD)
Float = 687.1 million shares
Monthly Chart

1981 1982 1983 1984 1985 1986 1987 1988 1989 1990 1991 1992 1993 1994 1995 1996

Chart created with SuperCharts® by Omega Research, Inc.

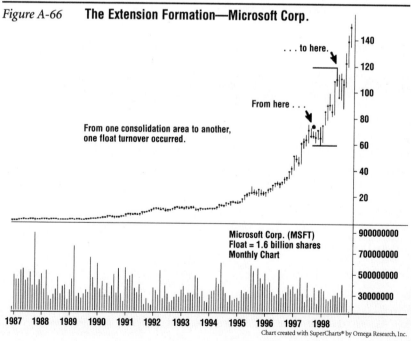

Figure A-66

The Extension Formation—Microsoft Corp.

. . . to here.

From here . . .

From one consolidation area to another,
one float turnover occurred.

Microsoft Corp. (MSFT)
Float = 1.6 billion shares
Monthly Chart

1987 1988 1989 1990 1991 1992 1993 1994 1995 1996 1997 1998

Chart created with SuperCharts® by Omega Research, Inc.

Figure A-67   The Extension Formation—Thermotrex Corp.

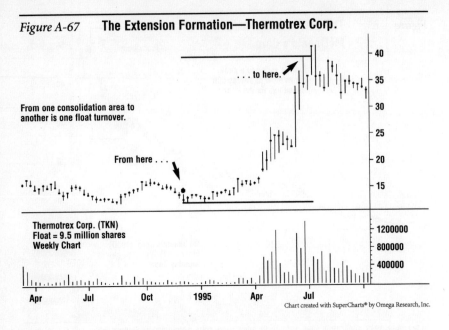

... to here.

From one consolidation area to
another is one float turnover.

From here . . .

Thermotrex Corp. (TKN)
Float = 9.5 million shares
Weekly Chart

Chart created with SuperCharts® by Omega Research, Inc.

Figure A-68   The Extension Formation—Online Systems Services Inc.

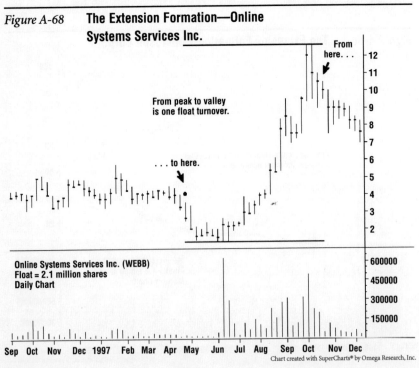

From
here . . .

From peak to valley
is one float turnover.

. . . to here.

Online Systems Services Inc. (WEBB)
Float = 2.1 million shares
Daily Chart

Chart created with SuperCharts® by Omega Research, Inc.

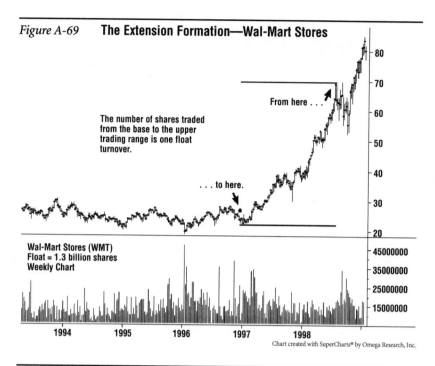

Figure A-69   The Extension Formation—Wal-Mart Stores

From here . . .

The number of shares traded
from the base to the upper
trading range is one float
turnover.

. . . to here.

Wal-Mart Stores (WMT)
Float = 1.3 billion shares
Weekly Chart

Chart created with SuperCharts® by Omega Research, Inc.

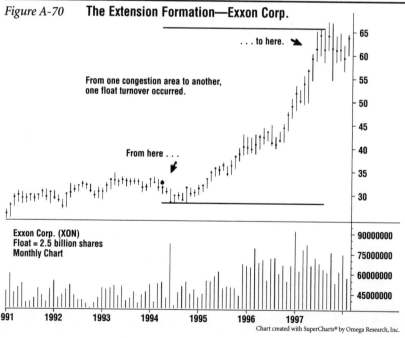

Figure A-70   The Extension Formation—Exxon Corp.

. . . to here.

From one congestion area to another,
one float turnover occurred.

From here . . .

Exxon Corp. (XON)
Float = 2.5 billion shares
Monthly Chart

Chart created with SuperCharts® by Omega Research, Inc.

DISCOVERY 8

The Upright Flag Formation

Price support in up-trends commonly occurs as a stock's price falls to the 50% point in the float turnover price range, giving rise to upright flag formations with a buy point.

Examples:

A-71   ACC Corp. (ACCC)
A-72   Media Arts (MDA)
A-73   Ascend Communications (ASND)
A-74   ATC Communications (ATCT)
A-75   Gibson Greetings Inc. (GIBG)
A-76   Pure World Inc. (PURW)
A-77   Saville Systems (SAVLY)
A-78   Surge Components (SRGE)
A-79   Telespectrum Worldwide (TLSP)
A-80   Online System Services Inc. (WEBB)

Figure A-71   **The Upright Flag Formation—ACC Corp.**

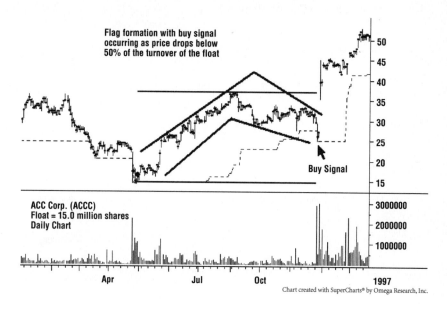

Flag formation with buy signal
occurring as price drops below
50% of the turnover of the float

Buy Signal

ACC Corp. (ACCC)
Float = 15.0 million shares
Daily Chart

Apr   Jul   Oct   1997

Chart created with SuperCharts® by Omega Research, Inc.

Figure A-72   **The Upright Flag Formation—Media Arts**

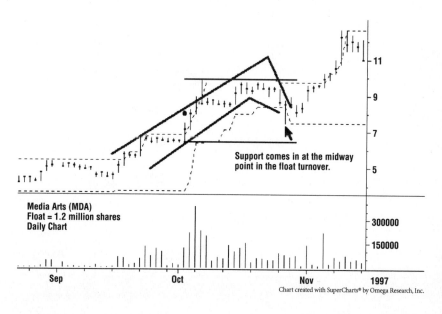

Support comes in at the midway
point in the float turnover.

Media Arts (MDA)
Float = 1.2 million shares
Daily Chart

Sep   Oct   Nov   1997

Chart created with SuperCharts® by Omega Research, Inc.

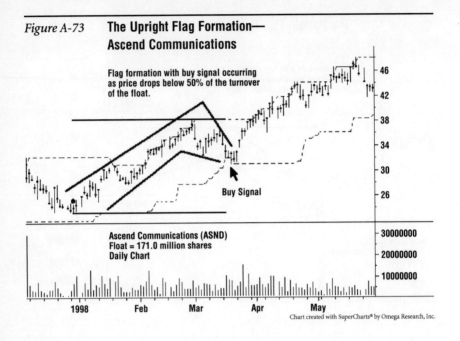

Figure A-73   **The Upright Flag Formation— Ascend Communications**

Flag formation with buy signal occurring as price drops below 50% of the turnover of the float.

Buy Signal

Ascend Communications (ASND)
Float = 171.0 million shares
Daily Chart

Chart created with SuperCharts® by Omega Research, Inc.

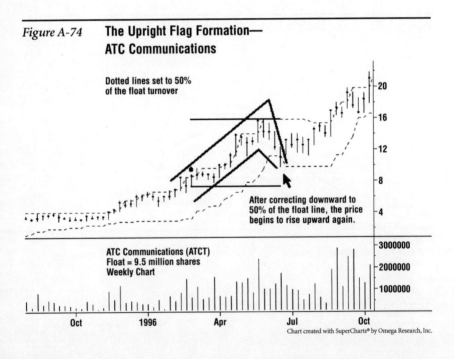

Figure A-74   **The Upright Flag Formation— ATC Communications**

Dotted lines set to 50% of the float turnover

After correcting downward to 50% of the float line, the price begins to rise upward again.

ATC Communications (ATCT)
Float = 9.5 million shares
Weekly Chart

Chart created with SuperCharts® by Omega Research, Inc.

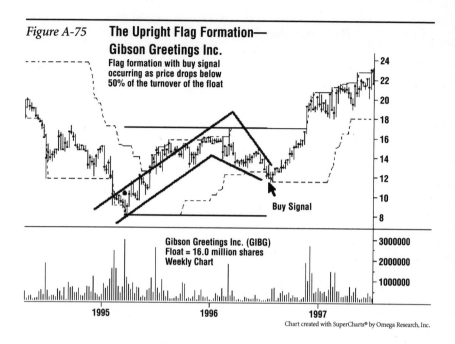

Figure A-75 **The Upright Flag Formation— Gibson Greetings Inc.**

Flag formation with buy signal occurring as price drops below 50% of the turnover of the float

Buy Signal

Gibson Greetings Inc. (GIBG)
Float = 16.0 million shares
Weekly Chart

Chart created with SuperCharts® by Omega Research, Inc.

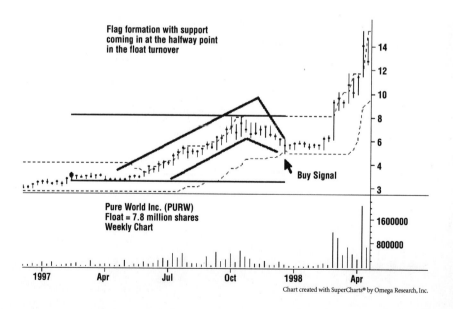

Figure A-76 **The Upright Flag Formation—Pure World Inc.**

Flag formation with support coming in at the halfway point in the float turnover

Buy Signal

Pure World Inc. (PURW)
Float = 7.8 million shares
Weekly Chart

Chart created with SuperCharts® by Omega Research, Inc.

Figure A-77   The Upright Flag Formation—Saville Systems

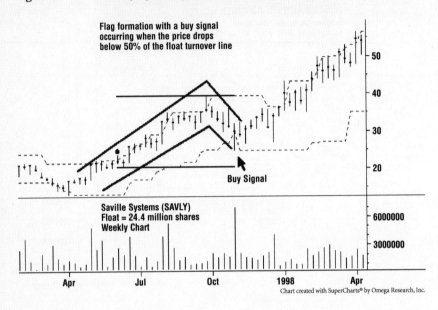

Flag formation with a buy signal occurring when the price drops below 50% of the float turnover line

Buy Signal

Saville Systems (SAVLY)
Float = 24.4 million shares
Weekly Chart

Chart created with SuperCharts® by Omega Research, Inc.

Figure A-78   The Upright Flag Formation—Surge Components

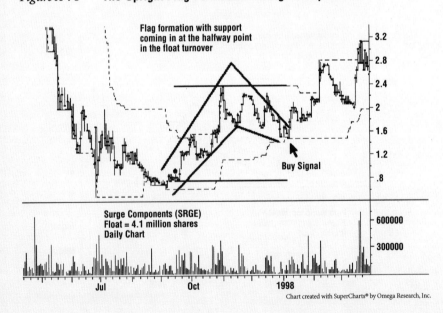

Flag formation with support coming in at the halfway point in the float turnover

Buy Signal

Surge Components (SRGE)
Float = 4.1 million shares
Daily Chart

Chart created with SuperCharts® by Omega Research, Inc.

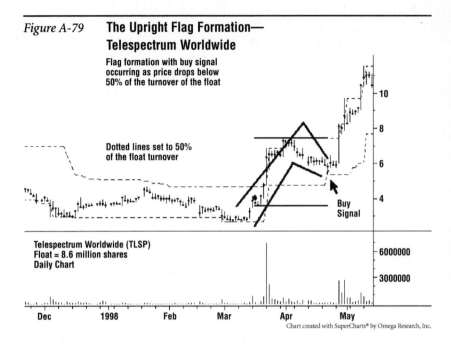

Figure A-79   **The Upright Flag Formation—Telespectrum Worldwide**

Flag formation with buy signal occurring as price drops below 50% of the turnover of the float

Dotted lines set to 50% of the float turnover

Buy Signal

Telespectrum Worldwide (TLSP)
Float = 8.6 million shares
Daily Chart

Chart created with SuperCharts® by Omega Research, Inc.

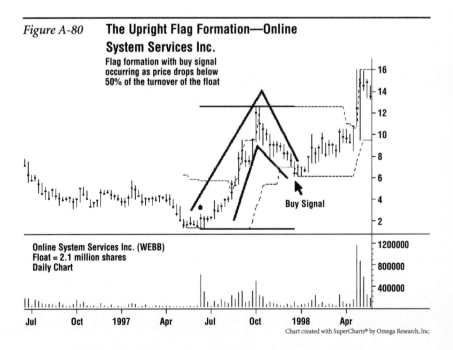

Figure A-80   **The Upright Flag Formation—Online System Services Inc.**

Flag formation with buy signal occurring as price drops below 50% of the turnover of the float

Buy Signal

Online System Services Inc. (WEBB)
Float = 2.1 million shares
Daily Chart

Chart created with SuperCharts® by Omega Research, Inc.

DISCOVERY 9

The Inverted Flag Formation

Price resistance in down-trends occurs as a stock's price rises to the 50% point in the float turnover price range, giving rise to inverted flag formations with a sell point.

Examples:

A-81   Catalyst Semiconductor (CATS)
A-82   Check Point Software (CHKP)
A-83   Cirrus Logic (CRUS)
A-84   C-Cube Inc. (CUBE)
A-85   Gourmet Brothers (BEAN)
A-86   Group Long Distance (GLDI)
A-87   IIVI Inc. (IIVI)
A-88   Information Research (IREG)
A-89   KCS Energy Inc. (KCS)
A-90   Photon Dynamics (PHTN)

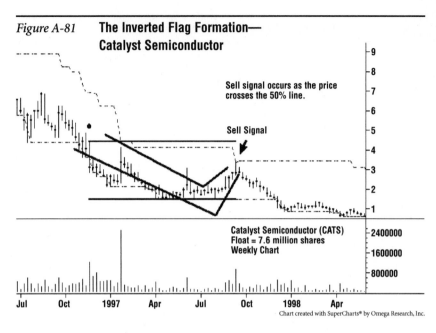

Figure A-81 **The Inverted Flag Formation—
Catalyst Semiconductor**

Sell signal occurs as the price
crosses the 50% line.

Sell Signal

Catalyst Semiconductor (CATS)
Float = 7.6 million shares
Weekly Chart

Chart created with SuperCharts® by Omega Research, Inc.

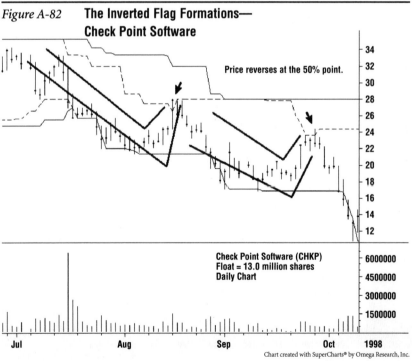

Figure A-82 **The Inverted Flag Formations—
Check Point Software**

Price reverses at the 50% point.

Check Point Software (CHKP)
Float = 13.0 million shares
Daily Chart

Chart created with SuperCharts® by Omega Research, Inc.

Figure A-83   **The Inverted Flag Formation—Cirrus Logic**

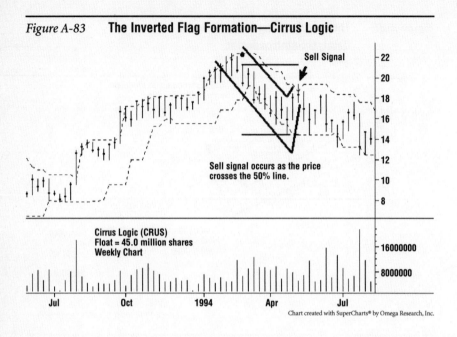

Sell Signal

Sell signal occurs as the price
crosses the 50% line.

Cirrus Logic (CRUS)
Float = 45.0 million shares
Weekly Chart

Jul   Oct   1994   Apr   Jul

16000000

8000000

Figure A-84   **The Inverted Flag Formation—C-Cube Inc.**

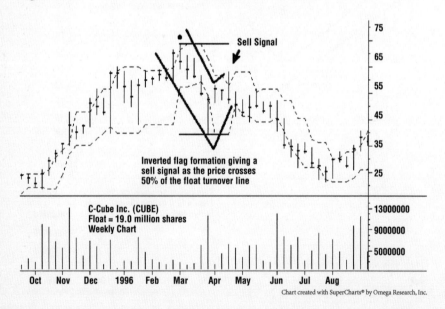

Sell Signal

Inverted flag formation giving a
sell signal as the price crosses
50% of the float turnover line

C-Cube Inc. (CUBE)
Float = 19.0 million shares
Weekly Chart

Oct   Nov   Dec   1996   Feb   Mar   Apr   May   Jun   Jul   Aug

13000000

9000000

5000000

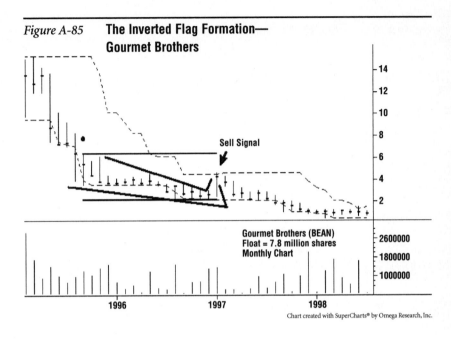

Figure A-85 **The Inverted Flag Formation—
Gourmet Brothers**

Sell Signal

Gourmet Brothers (BEAN)
Float = 7.8 million shares
Monthly Chart

Chart created with SuperCharts® by Omega Research, Inc.

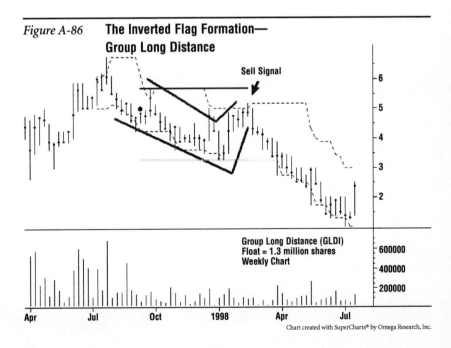

Figure A-86 **The Inverted Flag Formation—
Group Long Distance**

Sell Signal

Group Long Distance (GLDI)
Float = 1.3 million shares
Weekly Chart

Chart created with SuperCharts® by Omega Research, Inc.

Figure A-87 The Inverted Flag Formation—IIVI Inc.

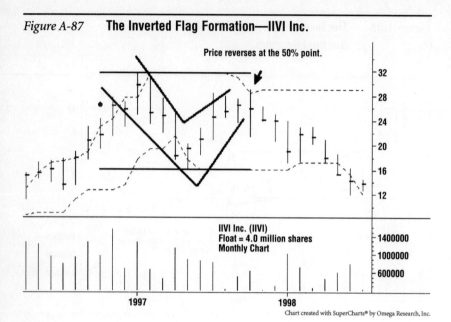

Price reverses at the 50% point.

IIVI Inc. (IIVI)
Float = 4.0 million shares
Monthly Chart

Chart created with SuperCharts® by Omega Research, Inc.

Figure A-88 The Inverted Flag Formation— Information Research

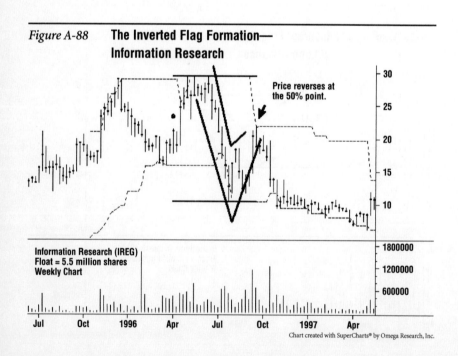

Price reverses at the 50% point.

Information Research (IREG)
Float = 5.5 million shares
Weekly Chart

Chart created with SuperCharts® by Omega Research, Inc.

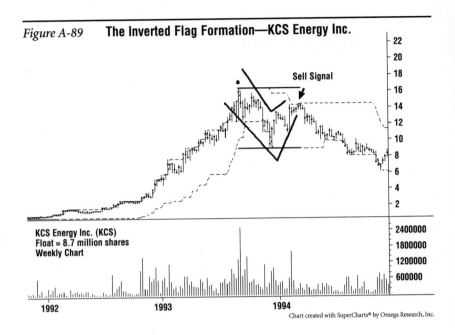

Figure A-89   **The Inverted Flag Formation—KCS Energy Inc.**

Sell Signal

KCS Energy Inc. (KCS)
Float = 8.7 million shares
Weekly Chart

1992   1993   1994

Chart created with SuperCharts® by Omega Research, Inc.

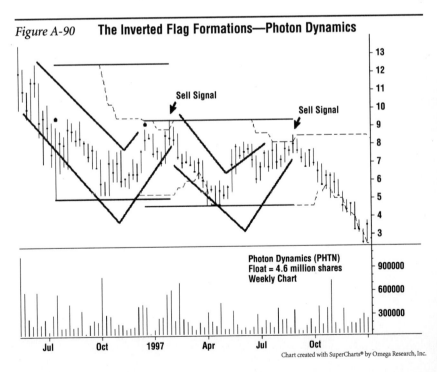

Figure A-90   **The Inverted Flag Formations—Photon Dynamics**

Sell Signal

Sell Signal

Photon Dynamics (PHTN)
Float = 4.6 million shares
Weekly Chart

Jul   Oct   1997   Apr   Jul   Oct

Chart created with SuperCharts® by Omega Research, Inc.

DISCOVERY 10

The Weak Base of Support Formation

Price resistance in down-trends following a topping formation occurs as a stock's price rises above the float turnover price range, thus giving rise to weak bases of support with a breakout to the upside sell point.

Examples:

A-91   ACC Corp. (ACCC)
A-92   Applix Inc. (APLX)
A-93   Catalyst Semiconductor (CATS)
A-94   Compare Generiks (COGE)
A-95   Cymer Inc. (CYMI)
A-96   Kulicke & Soffa Inds. (KLIC)
A-97   Panda Project Inc. (PNDA)
A-98   Semtech Corp. (SMTC)
A-99   Telebane Financial Corp. (TBFC)
A-100   Vocaltech Communications (VOCLF)

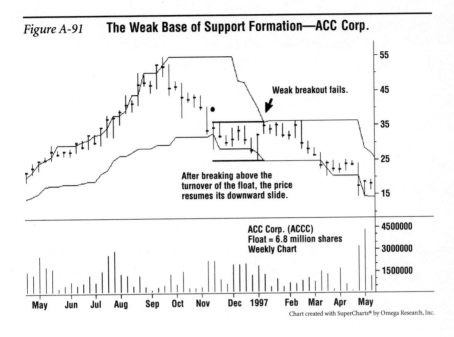

Figure A-91 **The Weak Base of Support Formation—ACC Corp.**

Weak breakout fails.

After breaking above the
turnover of the float, the price
resumes its downward slide.

ACC Corp. (ACCC)
Float = 6.8 million shares
Weekly Chart

Chart created with SuperCharts® by Omega Research, Inc.

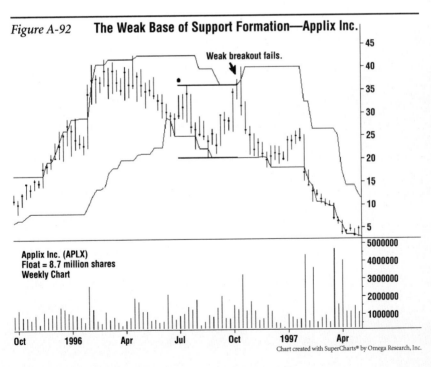

Figure A-92 **The Weak Base of Support Formation—Applix Inc.**

Weak breakout fails.

Applix Inc. (APLX)
Float = 8.7 million shares
Weekly Chart

Chart created with SuperCharts® by Omega Research, Inc.

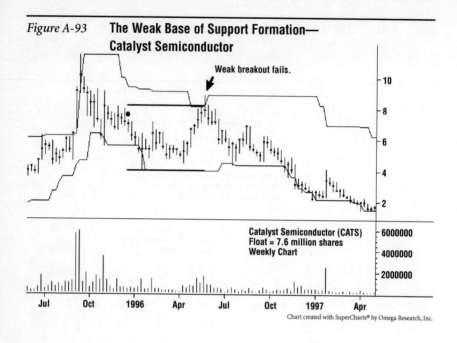

Figure A-93 **The Weak Base of Support Formation—
Catalyst Semiconductor**

Weak breakout fails.

Catalyst Semiconductor (CATS)
Float = 7.6 million shares
Weekly Chart

Chart created with SuperCharts® by Omega Research, Inc.

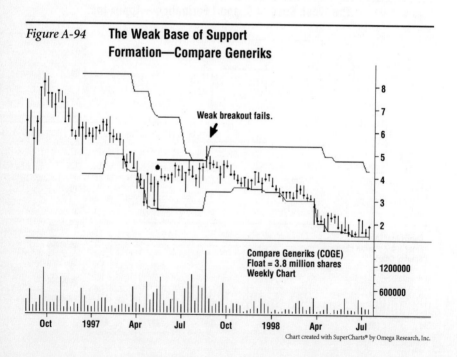

Figure A-94 **The Weak Base of Support
Formation—Compare Generiks**

Weak breakout fails.

Compare Generiks (COGE)
Float = 3.8 million shares
Weekly Chart

Chart created with SuperCharts® by Omega Research, Inc.

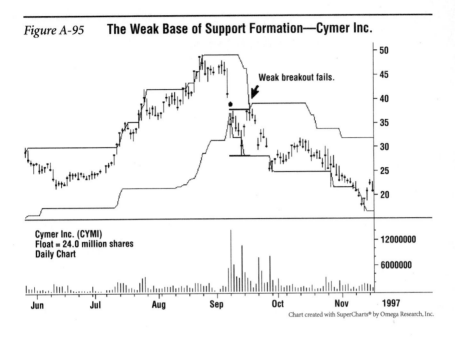

Figure A-95 **The Weak Base of Support Formation—Cymer Inc.**

Weak breakout fails.

Cymer Inc. (CYMI)
Float = 24.0 million shares
Daily Chart

Chart created with SuperCharts® by Omega Research, Inc.

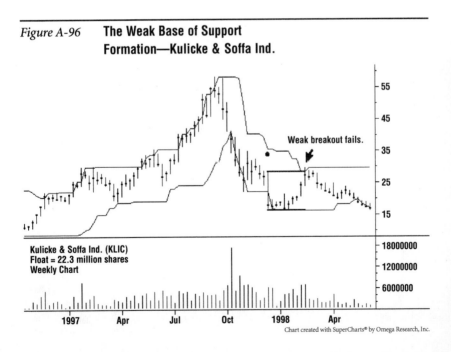

Figure A-96 **The Weak Base of Support Formation—Kulicke & Soffa Ind.**

Weak breakout fails.

Kulicke & Soffa Ind. (KLIC)
Float = 22.3 million shares
Weekly Chart

Chart created with SuperCharts® by Omega Research, Inc.

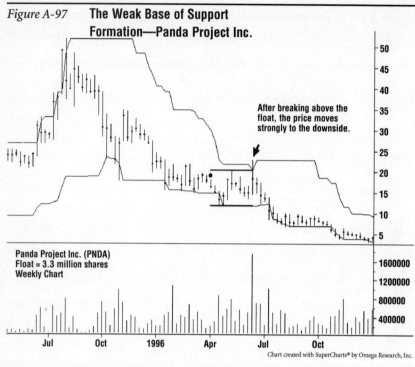

Figure A-97 **The Weak Base of Support Formation—Panda Project Inc.**

After breaking above the float, the price moves strongly to the downside.

Panda Project Inc. (PNDA)
Float = 3.3 million shares
Weekly Chart

Chart created with SuperCharts® by Omega Research, Inc.

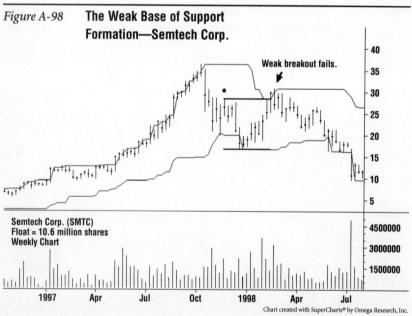

Figure A-98 **The Weak Base of Support Formation—Semtech Corp.**

Weak breakout fails.

Semtech Corp. (SMTC)
Float = 10.6 million shares
Weekly Chart

Chart created with SuperCharts® by Omega Research, Inc.

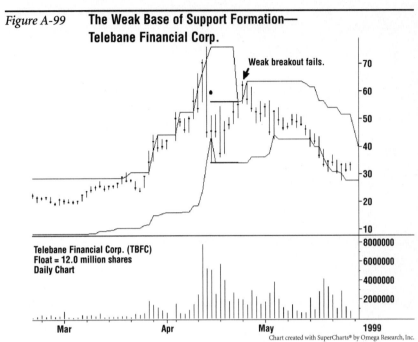

Figure A-99   **The Weak Base of Support Formation—
Telebane Financial Corp.**

Weak breakout fails.

70
60
50
40
30
20
10

Telebane Financial Corp. (TBFC)
Float = 12.0 million shares
Daily Chart

8000000
6000000
4000000
2000000

Mar   Apr   May   1999

Chart created with SuperCharts® by Omega Research, Inc.

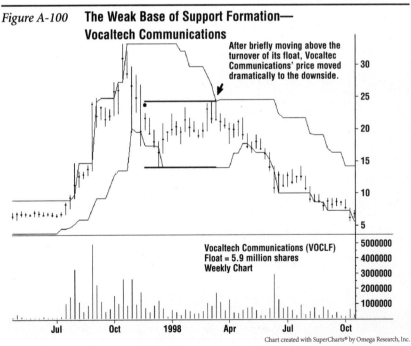

Figure A-100   **The Weak Base of Support Formation—
Vocaltech Communications**

After briefly moving above the
turnover of its float, Vocaltec
Communications' price moved
dramatically to the downside.

30
25
20
15
10
5

Vocaltech Communications (VOCLF)
Float = 5.9 million shares
Weekly Chart

5000000
4000000
3000000
2000000
1000000

Jul   Oct   1998   Apr   Jul   Oct

Chart created with SuperCharts® by Omega Research, Inc.

APPENDIX B

The Dilemma of Differing Results Resolved

When the cumulative-volume float indicator and the percentage float indicator are used to track the same stock, a curious phenomenon sometimes occurs, which was rather confusing when I first discovered it. One can get conflicting results about the amount of time it takes for a stock's float to go through one turnover. The problem occurs because the *float* indicator is adding volume backward and the *percentage* indicator is adding volume forward. Let me try to explain using a simple example: Imagine a stock with a float of 100 shares (highly improbable, but it will serve for explanatory purposes). Now imagine that on the first day of trading, 90 shares trade, and every day thereafter only five shares trade. If we use the percentage indicator, we start counting with the 90-share day and then add five and then add the next five. At this point, 100 shares have traded, which equals the float. So the float turnover is only three days long. But if we use the original float indicator, we are adding up numbers from right to left. Thus, we start with the most current day and add backward until the total reaches 100. In this case, we again reach a complete turnover when we get to the third day and add up the first three numbers. But look what happens on the fourth day. We now have to add the following numbers — 5, 5, 5, and 90. Remember we're counting backward until the total is equal to or greater than 100. Thus, on the fourth day of counting backward, the turnover is four days long but, actually, 105 shares have traded. On the fifth day we add 5, 5, 5, 5, and 90, and now the time of the turnover is five days long but 110 shares have actually traded. If we keep doing this, the float turnover on day 20 will be 20 days in length even

!

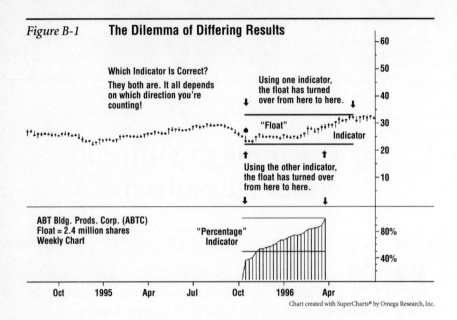

Figure B-1   The Dilemma of Differing Results

Which Indicator Is Correct?
They both are. It all depends on which direction you're counting!

Using one indicator, the float has turned over from here to here.

"Float" Indicator

Using the other indicator, the float has turned over from here to here.

ABT Bldg. Prods. Corp. (ABTC)
Float = 2.4 million shares
Weekly Chart

"Percentage" Indicator

Oct   1995   Apr   Jul   Oct   1996   Apr

Chart created with SuperCharts® by Omega Research, Inc.

though 195 (!) shares have traded hands. Finally, on day 21 when we add all our 5s, we only have 5s to add. We no longer have that big 90-day volume number in our calculation. Now the float of 100 shares shows up as trading in 20 days and, in fact, 100 shares did trade in 20 days.

A good example of this dilemma is seen in the chart of ABT Bldg. Prods. Corp. (ABTC) (see figure B-1).

Using the percentage indicator, the counting begins in the middle of October 1995 and adds forward in time. By the end of March 1996, we reach the float number of 2.4 million shares. Using the other indicator, the float indicator, we start counting backward from the date to the far right at the end of May 1996 and add up the numbers backward. This has the turnover going back to the percentage indicator's starting point in mid-October. Thus it would seem that we get two different readings on the time it takes for a float turnover to take place.

When I first came across this phenomenon, I wasn't sure how important it was. I knew that the concept of the float turnover was a hypothetical construct to begin with, but now it seemed that my primary measuring device could totally screw up the calculation. The resolution to the problem came when I realized that each indicator was designed for a specific purpose and, in fact, that purpose was still being fulfilled. The float indicator was designed to signal when the price goes above or below the float turnover. I wanted to be able to find stocks in long down-trends just when their prices moved above the float turnover. I also wanted to be able to find stocks in long up-trends just when their prices moved below the float turnover. This is exactly what the indicator does. The percentage indicator, on the other hand, was designed to sound an alert when a stock in an extension formation has its cumulative trading volume equal to its float, and that is exactly what it does.

We must remember that we cannot know the intentions of all the investors involved. Short-term players are moving in and out, and long-term players are holding through complete turnovers. Because the turnover is a hypothetical construct, we end up with a close approximation to the truth.

What absolutely amazes people who learn about float analysis is the degree of correspondence that occurs between the actual time it takes for a stock to make a basing pattern as well as the time it takes for a stock to become extended in price, and the hypothetical turnover that is produced by using these indicators. The charts themselves become things of beauty because they so clearly show this correspondence!

Remember, too, that since I am the first person (to my knowledge) to make and use these indicators, I am not only using them as trading tools, but I am also using them to show the correspondence that is so fascinating to observe.

Bibliography

Baruch, Bernard M. (1957). *Baruch, My Own Story.* Henry Holt and Company, New York, NY.

Darvas, Nicolas (1960). *How I Made Two Million Dollars in the Stock Market.* Lyle Stuart, Secaucus, NJ.

Edwards, Robert D., and Magee, John (1966). *Technical Analysis of Stock Trends.* John Magee Inc., Boston, MA.

Gann, W.D. (1976). *Truth of the Stock Tape.* Lambert-Gann Publishing, Pomeroy, WA.

Graham, Benjamin (1973). *The Intelligent Investor.* Harper & Row, New York, NY.

Graham, Benjamin and Dodd, David (1934). *Security Analysis.* McGraw-Hill, New York, NY.

Le Bon, Gustave (1973). *The Crowd.* Viking Press, New York, NY.

Lefevre, Edwin (1923). *Reminiscences of a Stock Operator.* George H. Doran and Company, New York, NY (reprint, with a foreword by Jack Schwager, John Wiley & Sons, Inc., New York, NY, 1993).

Livermore, Jesse L. (1940). *How to Trade in Stocks.* Traders Press, Greenville, SC.

Loeb, Gerald M. (1935). *The Battle for Investment Survival.* Fraser Publishing Company, Burlington, VT.

Lynch, Peter (1989). *One Up on Wall Street.* Penguin Books, New York, NY.

Mackay, Charles (1932). *Memoirs of Extraordinary Popular Delusions and the Madness of Crowds.* Farrar, Straus and Giroux, New York, NY.

O'Neil, William J. (1988). *How to Make Money in Stocks.* McGraw-Hill, New York, NY.

Pring, Martin J. (1985). *Technical Analysis Explained, The Successful Investor's Guide to Spotting Investment Trends and Turning Points.* McGraw-Hill, New York, NY.

Sperandeo, Victor (1991). *Trader Vic — Methods of a Wall Street Master.* John Wiley & Sons, Inc., New York, NY.

Stein, Lawrence M. (1988). *Value Investing, New Strategies for Stock Market Success.* John Wiley & Sons, Inc., New York, NY.

Warren, Ted (1966). *How to Make the Stock Market Make Money for You.* Four Star Books, Inc., Ojai, CA.

Weinstein, Stan (1988). *Stan Weinstein's Secrets for Profiting in Bull and Bear Markets.* Business One Irwin, Homewood, IL.

Zweig, Martin (1986). *Winning on Wall Street.* Warner Books, New York, NY.

Glossary

The following glossary is not meant to be a complete financial resource. It has been created only to help clarify the terms used in this book.

A

absolute bottom formation — the lowest historical price level containing a complete single float turnover and a breakout buy point.

absolute top formation — the highest historical price level containing a complete single float turnover and a breakout sell point.

accumulation — buying shares of stock with the intent of holding them. When all the shares available for trading are accumulated, any new buying will drive the price up. The opposite of distribution.

area of price congestion — a sideways price pattern in which prices stay within a trading range until they move away in either an upward or downward direction (*see* **base of support**).

analyst's upgrades and downgrades — recommendations to buy or sell a stock by an analyst at a major stock brokerage house.

B

base of support— a price chart pattern with prices moving sideways that precedes an upward move in prices. Also known as a basing area, basing formation, basing pattern, price consolidation area, and area of price congestion. In a float turnover bottom formation, the base of support corresponds exactly to the number of shares in the float (*see also* **rising base of support**).

bear market — a 20% or more decline in the prices of all the major indexes (Dow Jones Industrials, the S&P 500, and the NASDAQ Composite).

bottom formation — a U-shaped price and volume chart pattern in which all of a company's shares that are available for trading change hands *once* at the bottom of the U. One of the 12 most common of the price and volume chart patterns found in float analysis.

bottom picking — the analysis of stocks that have been going down in price with the hope of finding one for which the price will turn around and go higher.

bottom within a correction formation — a price and volume chart pattern in which all of a company's shares that are available for trading change hands once right at the bottom of the stock's price correction. One of the 12 most common of the price and volume chart patterns found in float analysis.

breakout — a rise in prices above a basing area.

breakout bar — that bar in which the price breaks above or below a basing price consolidation area.

broad market sell-off — *see* **major market correction** or **bear market**.

bull market — a substantial rise in prices in all the major indexes (Dow Jones Industrials, the S&P 500, and the NASDAQ Composite).

C

call option — a financial security that gives the owner the right to buy a certain number of shares of an underlying security at a fixed price over a fixed period of time.

ceiling of resistance — owners of stock who are holding losing positions and will sell into any rise in prices to break even. A ceiling of resistance is seen on charts with declining prices (*see also* **descending ceiling of resistance**).

channel lines — *see* **float channel lines**.

consolidation area — a sideways price pattern in which prices stay within a trading range until they move in either an upward or downward direction (*see* **base of support** *and* **ceiling of resistance**).

correction — a short-term price decline that occurs during a long-term price increase.

cumulative trading volume — the total number of shares traded over a given period of time. For example, if a stock traded 10 million shares one day and 9 million shares the next day, the cumulative trading volume for the two-day span would be 19 million shares.

cumulative-volume channel indicator — a stock indicator that shows the float turnover in a historical *channel-line* format. It does this by taking the highest and lowest prices reached during a float's turnover and tracking them on a continuum, or channel line basis. This indicator allows breakout points above or below the float turnover to be easily seen. Created by Steve Woods and Jan Arps.

cumulative-volume float indicator — a stock indicator that tracks the float turnover by adding volume numbers cumulatively in a *reverse* chronological direction starting from any given date. The end of the float is referenced by placing a dot above the bar in which a complete turnover has occurred. Two lines are added to reference the highest and lowest prices reached during the float's turnover and serve as trigger lines for price alerts. Created by Steve Woods and Jan Arps.

cumulative-volume percentage indicator — a histogram stock indicator that tracks the float turnover by adding volume numbers cumulatively in a *forward* chronological direction starting from any given date. It is plotted as a histogram on a percentage of the float basis. An alert can be given when one turnover of float is reached in the cumulative count. Created by Steve Woods and Jan Arps.

D

day trader — a very short-term trader who usually goes to cash at the end of each day.

descending ceiling of resistance — excess supply of a stock as its prices decline during a substantial time period; having a stock's price stay in the lowest region of a float turnover price range during a substantial price decline; having a large percentage of investors who are holding losing positions above the present price of a stock.

distribution — selling shares of stock with the intent of getting rid of them. When a stock is under distribution, its prices will soon go down.

down-trend — the tendency of a stock's price to continue moving in a downward direction.

down-trends — declining prices of various time durations: short-term down-trends last for hours, days, or weeks; medium-term down-trends last for weeks or months; and long-term down-trends last for months or years.

downward move — *see* **move to the downside.**

E

entry point — a buy point that will make an investor money.

exit point — a sell point that will make an investor money.

F

fast extension formation — a rapid increase in prices in which the distance from the base of support to the top of the price rise is one float turnover in length.

fast move to the upside — a rapid increase in prices over a short period of time.

fifty percent (50%) support point and 50% resistance point — a natural or inherent point of support and resistance found on float analysis chart formations. It is discovered by setting the cumulative-volume float and channel indicators to exactly half the number of the float for any given stock. The 50% support point is seen when prices correct downward and reverse direction just at the midway point in the float turnover. The 50% resistance point is seen when price retracements reverse direction just at the midway point in the float turnover.

float — all of a company's shares that are actually available for trading (i.e.,) the number of freely traded shares in the hands of the public. These shares are determined by subtracting the number of stocks held by a company's management from the total shares outstanding that a company has issued.

float (from cbs.marketwatch.com *Financial Glossary*)— the float is the number of shares of a security that are outstanding and available for trading by the public.

float (from *Daily Graphs*) — number of shares that are not closely held.

float (from *Investor's Business Daily*) — shares outstanding less stock owned by management.

float (from Yahoo!'s *Financial Glossary*) — (1) the number of shares that are actively tradable in the market, excluding shares that are held by officers and major stakeholders that have agreements not to sell until someone else is offered the stock. (2) this is the number of freely traded shares in the hands of the public. (Float is calculated as Shares Outstanding minus Shares Owned by Insiders, 5% Owners, and Rule 144 Shares.)

float analysis — a holistic approach to studying the technical behavior of stocks that treats the floating supply of shares as being equal in importance to *price* and *volume* activity for the purpose of making informed buying and selling decisions. A method that demonstrates a direct relationship between the volume of shares traded in the past and subsequent future movements in price.

float channel lines— continuum lines that plot the highest and lowest price range component of a stock's float turnover on a bar-to-bar basis. Channel lines allow the analyst to determine if the stock's price has been or is presently above, below, or within the float turnover's price range.

floating supply of shares — *see* **float**.

float turnover — the amount of time it takes for a number of shares to trade that cumulatively corresponds with the number of shares in the stock's float. For example, if a company's float has 100 million shares that are actively trading and the total cumulative volume of shares traded over the last year was 100 million shares, then a single float turnover would be a one-year span starting from the current date and going back to the day when the cumulative total of the volume equaled 100 million shares.

float turnover price range — the range of prices from the highest to lowest reached during a float turnover.

float turnover time range — the varying amount of time that it takes for a stock's floating supply of shares to trade hands once.

follow-through confirmation — price strength to the upside, occurring within a few days of a breakout.

fundamental analysis — studying a company's balance sheet to make informed buying and selling decisions. This approach to stock analysis focuses on such things as revenues, profits, profit margins, and overall market growth potential. One of two commonly used approaches to stock analysis; the other is **technical analysis**.

G

going short — borrowing stock and selling it in the open market with the hope of buying it back at a lower price. The goal is still buying low and selling high, except that one sells first and buys second.

H

higher high — a price bar on a stock chart where the highest price reached is higher than the highest price reached on the price bar immediately before it.

higher low — a price bar on a stock chart where the lowest price reached is higher than the lowest price reached on the price bar immediately before it.

I

indexes — groups of stocks whose prices are averaged together to get a broad feeling for the economy as a whole or various industry groups. The most commonly followed indexes are the Dow Jones Industrials, the S&P 500, and the NASDAQ Composite. Market technicians study the indexes closely in the attempt to increase investors' profitability.

industry group— all of the companies that sell a similar product. For example, the automotive industry group would include General Motors, Ford, Chrysler, Honda, Toyota, etc. The stocks of various industry groups are closely tracked in an attempt to determine which industry group is outperforming all the rest.

institutional players — stock market players with large amounts of money to invest (i.e., mutual funds and pension funds). The "big boys" who really drive a stock's price to higher levels. Strong stocks will always have the support of these players.

inverted flag formation — a price and volume chart formation that resembles an upside-down flag or pennant in which there is one float turnover. The formation is completed when the price finds resistance as it rises to the halfway point in the float turnover. From there, the price declines.

L

leadership — the best companies in the best industry groups. Bull markets always have those stocks that outperform all other stocks. Without leadership, there is a bear market.

legs to the downside — a drop in prices of the major market indexes (the Dow 30, the S&P 500, and the NASDAQ Composite) during a bear market or major market correction that is punctuated by sideways consolidation areas. A typical bear market will have two or three legs to the downside before making a major bottom. A typical major market correction will have one leg to the downside.

losing position — owning stock at a lower price than one paid for it.

lower high — a price bar on a stock chart where the highest price reached is lower than the highest price reached on the price bar immediately before it.

lower low — a price bar on a stock chart where the lowest price reached is lower than the lowest price reached on the price bar immediately before it.

M

MACD lines (moving average convergence divergence lines) — a technical stock indicator that uses a fast and a slowmoving average to determine when price up-trends and down-trends are beginning and ending.

major market correction — *see* **bear market**.

move to the downside — a decline in prices to lower and lower levels.

move to the upside — a rally in prices to higher and higher levels.

moving average line — the most commonly used of all technical stock indicators. It smooths out price volatility to show the direction of a stock's trend. It adds all the closing prices over a given period of time and averages them together. The resulting average is then plotted on the stock's price chart. The most commonly used moving averages are the 50-day and the 200-day.

multiple turnover base formation — a sideways price and volume chart formation found in float analysis in which the floating supply of shares goes through two or more complete turnovers.

N

new high ground — price increases to levels that have never been reached before.

O

one-day price reversal — (1) the day on which a series of daily upward price moves ends (i.e., the price reaches a higher high and a lower low but closes lower than the previous day's closing price). This type of one-day price reversal often signals the end of an upward price move. (2) the day in which a series of daily downward price moves ends (i.e., the price reaches a lower low and a lower high but closes higher than the previous day's closing price). This type of one-day price reversal quite often signals the end of a downward move.

one hundred percent (100%) resistance point — a price reversal point found on the *weak base of support* chart formation. It most often occurs after a stock has made a top formation and is beginning a long decline in price. The stock's price rises briefly above the float turnover and then reverses direction and heads downward. The reversal occurs because the buyers who bought the stock below this point are not holding their shares tightly, so the price begins to drop.

one hundred percent (100%) support point — a price reversal point found on the *overhead support* chart formation. It occurs when the price drops briefly below the float turnover and then reverses direction and heads up into new high ground. The reversal occurs because the buyers who bought the stock above this point are holding their shares tightly, so the price begins to rise.

open, high, low, close — a security's opening price, highest price reached, lowest price reached, and closing price for a given amount of time — daily, weekly, or monthly.

options — a financial security that gives the owner the right to buy or sell an underlying security at a set price for a certain amount of time. The option itself can also be traded for whatever the option is worth at any given time.

overhead base of support in an up-trend formation — a price and volume chart pattern in which all of a company's shares that are available for trading change hands once during a sideways price move that is part of a larger up-trend price move. Once all the shares have changed hands in the sideways price pattern, the price briefly drops below the float turnover and then begins to rise into new high ground. One of the 12 most common price and volume chart patterns found in float analysis.

overhead supply — owners of stock who are holding losing postions and will sell when the price comes back to the level at which they bought (*see* **resistance**).

P

price — the amount of money a stock is presently selling for or has sold for in the past.

price bar — a vertical line on a price and volume chart that can show the high, low, opening, and closing prices of a given security.

price component of a float turnover — the range of prices, highest and lowest, that a stock trades for during a float turnover. There are two ways that this price range can be shown on a price chart: (1) parallel lines that show not only the price range but also the time range of the float turnover; (2) channel lines that are created by plotting the highest and lowest points in the turnover and plotting these as single points above and below any individual bars on a chart. When these points are connected, they form a set of channel lines that show the price component on a historical basis and point to breakouts above and below the float turnover.

price consolidation area — when a stock's price goes sideways in a trading range. For example, a stock's price stays between $20 and $25 for several months and then runs to $60; when the price was in the trading range between $20 and $25, it was in a price consolidation area. The great discovery of float analysis is that it is quite common to find price consolidation areas to be exactly one float turnover in length. Price consolidation areas are also known as bases, bases of support, basing areas, basing formations, and areas of price congestion.

price extension — the rise or decline in prices away from a base of support.

price extension formations — a price and volume chart pattern in which all of a company's shares that are available for trading change hands once during an upward or downward move in prices as the price moves from one area of price congestion to another. A fast extension formation occurs in days or weeks. A slow extension formation occurs in weeks or months.

price reversal — a point where prices moving downward reverse direction and begin moving upward or prices that are moving upward reverse direction and begin to move downward.

price swings — the normal fluctuations in stock prices in which prices that are moving upward tend to move downward for short periods of time and prices that are moving downward tend to move upward for short periods of time.

put option — a financial security that gives the owner the right to sell a certain number of shares of an underlying security at a fixed price over a fixed period of time.

R

rally — a strong rise in prices, the opposite of a **correction**.

relative strength — the price performance of a stock over a given period of time compared to all other stocks in the stock market over the same period of time.

resistance — any point on a stock chart where owners of stock who are holding losing positions will sell into rising prices to break even.

retracement — an upward movement in prices that occurs for a brief period of time during a long-term price decline.

reversal—*see* **price reversal**.

rising base of support — strong demand for a stock as its price rises higher during a substantial time period; having a stock's price stay in the upper region of a float turnover price range during a substantial price increase; having a larger percentage of investors who are holding winning positions under the present price of a stock.

S

selling short — *see* **going short**.

shares outstanding — the total number of shares issued by a company.

slow extension formation — a slow increase in price in which the distance for the base of support to the top of the price rise is one float turnover in length. One of the 12 most common price and volume chart patterns found in float analysis.

stochastics — a technical stock indicator developed by Dr. George Lane based on the idea that prices in an up market tend to close at the top of their trading range and stocks in a down market tend to close at the bottom of their trading range.

straddle — an options trading strategy in which the trader buys both a put and a call option at the same time. The trader will make money if the underlying stock makes a major move in either direction from the strike price but will lose if the stock goes sideways.

strike price — the price at which an option can be bought or sold.

strong base — *see* **base of support**.

strong base of support in an up-trend formation — a price and volume chart pattern in which all of a company's shares that are available for trading change hands once during a sideways price move that is part of a larger up-trend price move. Once all the shares have changed hands in the sideways price pattern, the price rises into new high ground. One of the 12 most common price and volume chart patterns found in float analysis.

support — having plenty of buyers who are willing to buy the stock at any given level; the demand created by the buying public that pushes a stock's price upward; a point on a stock's price and volume chart at which buyers are plentiful and the stock, if moving downward, now begins to move upward (*see also* **base of support** and **rising base of support**).

swings in a sideways market — the up and down price fluctations that occur when a stock is forming a base of support or a ceiling of resistance.

T

taking a position — buying shares of any given stock.

technical analysis of stocks — the study of price and volume charts with the intention of finding profitable entry and exit points.

time component in a float turnover — the amount of time it takes for a number of shares to trade that corresponds exactly with the number of shares in a stock's float. When cumulatively counting backward from a given date, the length of the float turnover is marked in float analysis charts by a dot above the bar where the cumulative total of shares traded corresponds exactly with the stock's float. The time component can also be shown by two parallel lines, set to the highest and lowest prices reached in the float turnover. These lines extend from any given date backward to the price bar where the cumulative total corresponds exactly with the number of shares in the float.

top formation — an upside-down U-shaped price and volume chart pattern in which, right at the top, the number of shares traded corresponds with the number of shares in the float. One of the 12 most common price and volume chart patterns found in float analysis.

trend — the tendency in stock prices to continue moving in either an upward or downward direction (*see* **up-trend** and **down-trend**).

trigger lines — lines on a stock's price and volume chart that signal alerts when the stock's price crosses them.

turnover of the float — a time and price measurement of the floating supply of shares. The amount of time it takes for a specific number of shares to trade hands once, where the number of shares traded corresponds exactly with the number of shares in the float. Its price component refers to the the range of prices, highest and lowest reached, during the specified time frame. Commonly seen at bottom and top formations, it implies a change in ownership of the stock. It is the study of the float turnover on which float analysis is based. *see* **float turnover.**

U

upright flag formation — a price and volume chart formation that resembles a flag or pennant in which one float turnover occurs. The formation is completed when the price finds support when it drops to the halfway point in the float turnover. From there, the price rises.

up-trend — the tendency in a stock's price to continue moving in an upward direction.

up-trends — rising prices of various time durations. Short-term up-trends last for hours, days, or weeks; medium-term up-trends last for weeks or months; and long-term up-trends last for months or years.

upward move — *see* **move to the upside.**

V

valid breakout trading point — a buying or selling opportunity that would have made money for an investor who had taken the position.

valid breakout above a strong base of support — a rise in prices above a strong base of support in which the price continues to rise substantially.

valid breakout below a ceiling of resistance — a drop in prices below a weak base of support in which prices continue to drop substantially.

volume — the number of shares that are traded in any given time period.

W

Wall Street's Holy Grail — the idea that a secret, little-known technical approach of studying price and volume charts can produce profits consistently.

W. D. Gann — a famous stock market speculator of the 1930s, '40s, and '50s who used technical analysis of price and volume charts.

weak base of support — a sideways move in prices that is unable to support a rise in prices and leads to a decline.

weak base of support in a down-trend formation — a price and volume chart formation that has prices moving sideways for one complete float turnover and is unable to support a rise in prices. A rise in price above this formation is followed by declining prices.

winning position — owning stock at a higher price than one paid for it.

TRADING RESOURCE GUIDE

Tools for Success in Trading

Suggested Reading List

The W.D. Gann Method of Trading
by Gerald Marisch

Introductory work puts Gann's work in clear, usable terms. Great for traders trying to learn more about Gann's method of trading. Over 70 charts show the method in use.

Pattern, Price, and Time: Using Gann Theory in Trading Systems
by James Hyerczyk

Here's the first book to simplify Gann's concepts and apply them to all major markets. Also shows how to integrate Gann theory into modern computer charting systems.

The Arms Index (Trin Index)
by Richard Arms Jr.

Get an in-depth look at how volume, not time, governs market price changes. Describes the Arms short-term trading index (TRIN), a measure of the relative strength of the volume in relation to advancing stocks against that of declines.

Profits in Volume: Equivolume Charting
by Richard Arms Jr.

This method places emphasis on the trading range and trading volume, which are considered to be the two primary factors involved in technical analysis. They give an accurate appraisal of the supply and demand factors that influence a stock. Then you can determine if a stock is moving with ease or difficulty and, thereby, make better, more on-target investing decisions.

Technical Analysis of Stock Trends, 7th edition
by Robert D. Edwards and John Magee

A universally acclaimed classic, updated with the latest data in market performance and trends, on which the foundation of all technical analysis is built. Step-by-step coverage thoroughly explains and applies the current data.

Technical Analysis of the Financial Markets
by John Murphy

From how to read charts to understanding indicators and the crucial role of technical analysis in investing, you won't find a more thorough or up-to-date source. This is a must-have reference, from the industry expert.

Reminiscences of a Stock Operator
by Edwin Lefevre

Generations of investors have benefited from this 1923 masterpiece. Jack Schwager's new introduction explains why this account of Jesse Livermore, one of the greatest speculator's ever, continues to be the most widely read book in the trading community.

Extraordinary Popular Delusions and the Madness of Crowds & Confusion de Confusiones
by Charles Mackay and Andrew Tobias

These are the most important books ever written on crowd psychology and the financial markets. Featured on most top 10 lists of financial books, these classics explore the impact of crowd behavior, manias, and trading trickery in the market.

McMillan on Options
by Lawrence G. McMillan

It's the brand new bible of the options market. The world's leading expert on options gives a complete game plan for trading options. Here are McMillan's greatest strategies complete with precise instructions about how and when to use them.

Options as a Strategic Investment
by Lawrence G. McMillan

It's the top selling options book of all time, exhaustive coverage of every aspect of trading options. Called "the single most important options reference available," this mammoth work teaches you to track volatility, learn rules for entering and exiting trades at optimal levels, and build a successful trading plan.

Encyclopedia of Technical Market Indicators
by Robert W. Colby and Thomas A. Meyers

The most comprehensive description of technical indicators, including over 110 studies fully detailed. Endless examples plus a full commentary by the authors on how reliable each indicator is.

Technical Analysis Simplified
by Clif Droke

Here's a concise manual for learning and implementing this invaluable investment tool. The author distills the most essential elements of technical analysis into a brief, easy-to-read volume.

Point and Figure Charting: Essential Applications for Forecasting and Tracking Market Prices
by Thomas J. Dorsey

The first new work on point and figure in 30 years. Today's leading expert shows how to use point and figure to chart price movements on stocks, options, futures, and mutual funds. Learn to interpret the point and figure charts and recognize patterns that signal outstanding opportunities. Also covers how to combine point and figure with technical analysis for unbeatable success.

Martin Pring's Introduction to Technical Analysis: A CD-ROM Seminar and Workbook
by Martin J. Pring

The foremost expert on technical analysis and forecasting financial markets gives you a one-on-one course in every aspect of technical analysis.

This interactive guide explains how to evaluate trends, highs and lows, price and volume relationships, price patterns, moving averages, and momentum indicators. The CD-Rom includes videos, animated diagrams, audio clips, and interactive tests. It's the user-friendly way to master technical analysis from an industry icon.

Internet Sites

Traders' Library Bookstore . . . . **www.traderslibrary.com**
The number 1 source for trading and investment books, videos, audios, and software.

Steve Woods . . . . **www.floatanalysis.com**
Visit this site if you are interested in contacting Steve Woods or learning more about float analysis.

Jan Arps' Traders Toolbox . . . . **www.janarps.com.**
Purchase the Woods Cumulative-Volume Float Indicators, which are used solely on Omega Research's TradeStation and SuperCharts software.

Lawrence G. McMillan . . . . **www.optionstrategist.com**
Learn more about the latest techniques and strategies for trading a variety of innovative options products. You'll also discover hundreds of techniques to help you maximize your earning potential and minimize risk.

Martin Pring . . . . **www.pring.com**
This site is dedicated to teaching the art of technical analysis and charting.

Chicago Board of Options Exchange . . . . **www.cboe.com**
Daily market statistics with extensive archives and introduction to options.

Newsletters of Interest to Traders

Daily Option Strategist
Editor, Lawrence G. McMillan
www.optionstrategist.com

Dow Theory Letters
Editor, Richard Russell
www.dowtheoryletters.com

Option Advisor
Editor, Bernie Schaffer
www.optionadvisor.com

Option Strategist
Editor, Lawrence G. McMillan
www.optionstrategist.com

Stock Market Cycles
Editor, Peter Eliades
www.stockmarketcycles.com

Index

Page references for charts are set in italic type.